THE SECRET OF CHRIST

The Secret Of Christ – The Christos Code
By Michael Feeley

Published 2016 by Sazmick Books
Web: www.sazmickbooks.com
Web: www.michael-feeley.com

Book and Cover Design - Sarah Feeley

British Library Cataloguing-in Publication Data.
A catalogue record for this book is available from the British Library.

ISBN: 978-0-9954554-5-0

Printed and bound in the UK
using sustainable resources

SB SAZMICK BOOKS

THE SECRET OF CHRIST

MICHAEL FEELEY

SAZMICK BOOKS

OTHER TITLES BY MICHAEL FEELEY

Walk Into The Light – The Journey Of A Lightworker Duo
ISBN; 978-0-9566103-0-0

Beyond The Illusion – A Time Of Awakening
ISBN; 978-0-9566103-1-7

Earth Is An Experiment, Duality Is A Game... And Love Is The Answer
ISBN; 978-0-9566103-2-4

Available to purchase from

www.sazmickpublishing.com

ACKNOWLEDGEMENTS

My thanks go out to my wife Sarah for many things including your assistance in naming, designing and publishing of this book and also to the beautiful 'G' who I hope will one day read it; for your continued support and entertainment. Thanks also go out to family and friends and to Paul D Mamigonian, the author of the foreword of this book and my partner in other ventures outside hereof.

CONTENTS

FOREWORD:

By Author & Radio broadcaster Paul D Mamigonian:

This makes perfect sense, I'll continue listening, not that I have a choice as moving from my computer screen is now not an option. I cannot believe what I'm hearing, who are these people? Wait stop; did they just say "ex police persons". I'm hooked, you got me, such is your pull you have my complete attention, however I'm going to fight this and wriggle in the murky depths of my unknowing. If I come up now, I know my life will be thrust forward and there'll be no turning back. I could stay cloaked, wrapped in the chrysalis of ignorance, or I could break free, lifted on your words, evolving with my new found wings of knowledge.

I have to get these people on my radio show I thought. Such was Michael and Sarah Feeley's presence, I felt instantly acquainted with them. Contact made, we agreed to broadcast a show together. I wanted to hear again first hand their life story. Show night. I recall being held almost in a state of levitation from words so powerful, from life lessons so uplifting that the dimly lit studio had no confinement over me, indeed the city of Manchester had no longer such grip, for I had transcended, the listeners had transcended, my two co-hosts opposite displaying open mouthed expressions had transcended. One co-host held up a note with the words "DO NOT CUT TO A BREAK!!!". I nodded back in agreement and mouthed silently the words "These people are amazing". Juggling the mixer board, I had received many emailed questions from listeners, and also had many of my own of which I had managed to scribble down. My immediate quandary, do I put forward my questions or dismiss my selfishness and opt instead to submit the questions of the engrossed listeners. These people are speaking to and for us all, they have to be heard by everyone I thought as I watched the flashing screen alerts from the listeners. One extremely quick hour and thirty minutes later our time slot had almost finished, I brought to a close the show, thus ending the call with Michael and Sarah. Travelling home I felt like I had unearthed a treasure of great importance. Many emails of which I hadn't had time to read circulated in my mind, one in particular which pointed to the fact that anyone who takes a leap of faith has to be commended.

To leave a stable job and income as Michael and Sarah had, because it was at odds to their core beliefs and morals, well there aren't really enough hats to take off in respect. From that point on we became good friends and broadcast many shows together. Michael spoke at one of the stations conferences putting forward his research and findings to an enthralled gathering. Michael has a natural ability to express opinions and facts in a digestible manner, which leads the viewer, listener, reader to question their own reasoning and beliefs therefore gaining new understandings. With the purity of open mindedness, Michael has been able to evolve to greater levels, at a pace that can only be achieved by continued resonance to a higher self.

Now, "Cometh the hour, cometh the man" never a truer word spoken, and so it can be said with the anticipated and timely arrival of Michael's new book - *The Secret of Christ - The Christos Code*

We find ourselves at the most pivotal age in history, with each major cross road in time; we have been guided by the wisdom of prophetic sages. Confucius, Epictetus, Pythagoras, Thomas Aquinas, Aristotle. With the introduction of this book, we will come to appreciate Michael Feeley and place him rightly alongside these great men, a sage of the modern era. What you are about to read will forever echo on through the ages and live in you. *The Secret of Christ - The Christos Code,* looks passed the indoctrination of the church, and into the oppressive control enforced by the ruling elite all of which have laid comfortably spooning together in the bed of their worldwide deception. Michael writes with Knowledge, with Love, aiming to bring the oppressed masses together. What you are holding in your hands right now is a literary key to freedom.

Michael You have the floor.

With Love, Paul D Mamigonian.

ABOUT THE AUTHOR

Michael Feeley is an ex police officer who was based in the UK for 17 years.

He had always had an open mind but after meeting his Wife Sarah in 2006, also a police officer at the time, other worldly events and experiences took them away from the path they were walking and they suddenly found themselves in a world beyond this one. This ultimately led the pair to change direction in life and they took the decision to leave their careers in the police service, a move that is very rarely heard of in that kind of 'job for life' environment.

In 2009 Michael, along with his Wife, relived the murder of a Victorian teenager who had been suffocated by her stepfather in the year 1850, both were spirit attachments who had been lost in limbo in a realm of time gone by until the current modern day (This is described in the pair's first book 'Walk Into The Light'). This event turned both Michael and Sarah's world upside down and they awoke to the realisation that the majority of what we are taught and brought up to believe is quite often false, that there are many more existences out there that touch the fringes of our own and that we sometimes catch a glimpse of, or become a scene in the movie of. This event was followed by continuous sightings of unorthodox craft in the skies, both day and night, dimensional gateways opening up before their eyes at both ground level and in the sky, Angelic visitations and many other 'super-natural' events that continued to expand the levels of Michael's conscious awareness.

In 2009 at his first guided meditation Michael was shown a Golden key, which is the symbol of secret ancient knowledge and wisdom. He has also been shown a Red Rose manifesting out of the ceiling of his room which again means ‘impending spiritual wisdom, and he continues even to this day to see the number 22 in various sequences; again this is the numeric symbol of ancient knowledge. And this is exactly what has happened over many years. “It is a raging passion for me to learn and understand the hidden knowledge and language of the initiates and I have spent many years doing just that; filled with privilege to know; almost a return to where I may have left off elsewhere in another ancient time”. Michael spends his time amongst other things re-searching and expanding his knowledge and understanding of many alternative subjects and does his best to share what he learns with others. The information he has uncovered isn’t for everyone, but for those open minded enough to hear it out, they will get a multileveled insight into the world of hidden languages.

Michael along with Sarah runs his own publishing company, Sazmick Books Publishing, and is also the host of Sazmick Books Radio. For this latest book, *The Secret of Christ - The Christos Code* Michael and his Wife have broken from their usual tradition with Michael solely re-searching and writing the content, and Sarah designing and publishing the final product. Those years of learning will now be abbreviated and condensed into this book; Michael’s fourth, to show a greater realm that few will ever realise. It is a scientific alternative view based on the deep research undertaken; this is scientific fact, not merely a system of belief. It is hoped that you will enjoy what you are about to read and are able to take something from it, however big or small.

Open the door to many hidden secrets and walk armed with a new knowledge that has been supressed for many thousands of years. As author of the Da Vinci Code Dan Brown said “Symbols are very adept at hiding the truth”

The doors are about to be unlocked. . .

INTRODUCTION

Christ is the most famous character the world has ever known, worshipped by the global masses who dedicate their everyday lives to his name. But was he ever a real person who walked the Earth over 2000 years ago? Could there be a better explanation as to his existence and could it be much deeper than anyone has ever been taught? Could there be a much deeper meaning far greater than the physical entity in human form? In this book i offer astronomical, genetic and scientific evidence to highlight that for milleniums of our time we have been lied to and deceived by a ruling class of aristocracy intent on keeping the masses as far away from the light as they can by promoting fakse teachings that lead us away from the truth, the truth that we are micro Gods in our own right. I am not saying that Christ doesn't exist, in fact to the contrary, but what i am saying is that Christ exists in a different way to that taught in Churches and schools et al. The Christ as you will read and discover is the source of life on this planet , but that source is not a man! The physical story of a man is a manmade creation. The whole story is a code to hide a deeper truth that is also true of all religions of the world. It was once said by Pope Leo X that "It Has Served Us Well' This Myth Of Christ"...

We all have one thing in common however; a fact they try so hard to keep away from us. We have a body network that can ascend us to the higher places of existence known as our chakra system. The title of this book is significant in this way which is the secret of our own Christ within. The secret is secretion from our Pineal Glands which connects to our Christos, meaning 'relating to Christ'(the Crown Chakra) that in turn connects to the cosmos, it is our celestial receptor.

This book intends to show you that there is an agenda at play on the world stage and who is behind it and why. Religion is just one link of a long chain used against us all but it has been very successful and it has been cleaverly interwoven into the fabric of our lives.

Without further adeiu I will explain.

Religion; or as it should be stated, Religare, to hold back, to return to bondage; tells a story in itself. People the world over have been held under the bondage of belief for thousands of years, belief that their god is the only god, that their religion is the only correct religion and that all others are wrong.

There are about 30,000 denominations of Christianity alone and all state that they are right. This figure doesn't include the many other belief systems throughout the world. Why does humanity keep reaching without when all that they could ever need is within, within themselves, not in Temples, not in Churches, not in the Mosques and not within the Synagogues? Church derives from the word Circe, who was a goddess who invited men into her home and then stole their minds, no coincidence there, that's exactly what churches do. Our own Temple in the head, temple meaning God's house; is our own Golgotha, the place of skulls, the higher mind, the only place we need to look, but it is often where our Christ consciousness is condemned to death, just like the mythical Jesus. We will go into Jesus and how he is really a planetary existence later on in the book.

Religion is really Astrotheology, the worship of the 7 visible planets: Sun; Venus; Mars; Saturn; Moon; Jupiter; Mercury, which extends into the creation of the body universe.

Geometric Creation

Each religion worships one or a combination of these planets which we will detail later on. The ancients were expert astrologers they were masters, master meaning 'Measurer of stars'. We have a society based on astronomical language and words such as disaster, meaning Bad star, youngster meaning young star and of course Hollywood where we have A listers, which are 'A list stars', common naked eye stars seen every evening. They are the cast; c(ast), ast =star. The Druids used the wood from the Holly Tree to make their magic wands and therefore we have the magic of Hollywood. Dru is Oak and Id (wid) means to know, Druid therefore means oak/tree knowledge and tree derives from true 'true knowledge'. They also had connections to the mystery schools of Egypt and the Djedhi.

Over the coming chapters we will show you how our belief systems were deliberately created to throw humanity off the true greatness of themselves, to forever look outside and not within. We are human; we are supernatural gods; who need look no further than their own body which is the universe incarnate. The bible and other such books are multi-layered, at their superficial levels we get the church teachings; the falsity of physical people and characters who walked the Middle East and fed the masses with fish and loaves. But at their deepest levels we then begin to understand that the body and universe are connected by astronomy and medical astronomy and that the bible is really referring to our cosmic connection covered up so brilliantly by the "Greatest Story Ever Told" or should we say the greatest work of fraudulent fiction, sold and bought by the blindness of ignorance and desire to be told rather than to learn the facts for themselves; people of the book as they are commonly known, due to their reliance on religious material in the form of the bible and alike.

Some people however need the safety net of belief, passing the responsibility to an outside force to put the wrongs right. To some it is an essential comfort system to believe that salvation will come from without, it won't, it will only come from within, from within themselves.

There are so many people not asking valid questions such as if Jesus died for our sins, to wipe the slate clean for humanity then why are we still going to confession? If God created the Sun on the 4th day, how was it the 4th day? If the spirit cannot burn why should we be concerned about hell, and most importantly, where is the evidence other than words written hundreds of years after these characters were meant to have existed? As a consequence it is likely that there could not have been any accuracy of the facts, only guess work, or in this, and many other cases, nothing more than a mere story.

There are good people within the world of belief, they are beautiful souls, but they have been duped. Some desire for truth, some believe they have found it and need look no further, but our consciousness level as a race hasn't progressed in many thousands of years because we are still clinging onto ancient manufactured beliefs and belief systems put in place by those of a higher knowledge base to keep us away from the path of enlightenment and truth.

But after many years of research and guided knowledge it is quite apparent that no such bible characters existed, not in physical form in any case. All biblical stories have an astronomical or medical astronomical base. It will also become apparent that the deaths of certain prominent individuals like Princess Diana were also timed in line with planetary alignments and numerological significance and were therefore no accident. And this is also correct with the likes of many terrorist events such as 9/11.

I hope that you enjoy the esoteric revelations in this book and that it makes the reader desire to look deep, look within and look beyond and find the knowledge that has been kept from us for far too long.

As in the Cain and Abel story, Cain being the custom, the accepted way of behaving and Abel meaning to speak out against it, this book does just that, it speaks out against societies lies and deception, the battle of dark and light. There are many characters in the bible named Simon, or in Hebrew Shimon, meaning to hear. Many won't want to hear the contents of this book.

Well done and thank you to those who do. The book is short and succinct and to the point, and leaves space for the readers to further the research for themselves with this book as a stepping stone and foundation upon which to build.

In the words of George Bernard Shaw *"All great truths begin as blasphemies"*

"Religion was created when the first conman met the first fool" - Mark Twain.

Verse I.O

IN THE BEGINNING WAS THE WORD

There are far too many biblical stories to be covered and analysed in one book, but we will cover the most well-known events that are practised and spoken about in modern day society. I will show how those stories are really referring to both an astronomical and bodily synergy, not physical people which we have previously mentioned is little more than a smoke-screen, a red herring to steer you away from knowledge taught and known only by the initiates to be used for their own advantage. Religion is a deliberate divide and control system to keep humanity fighting against each other. All religions have a form of worship but when we look into the origin of words we see that worship derives from war-ship and ship means to divide; just like the water does when a ship passes through. That is exactly what has happened to humanity, we have become divided by beliefs given to us, achievable by virtue of that fact we don't question or challenge anything, we just accept and that is our downfall. Until now that is!

Our universe, meaning one verse, the mathematical equation based on the metre, is the combination of light, sound, harmonics and mathematics. As Pythagoras once proclaimed "All is number". Numbers are also contained within the biblical scripture such as the 'Chariots of fire' which are myriads, the representation of the highest ancient number of 10,000.

Everything has a number sequence, vortex mathematics enters our realm to create the Torus, the spiral from which things stem, from the universe to our body as it goes through the 64 tetrahedron grid of birth in sequences of 8. The

Fibonacci sequence is nature's code, the spiral that creates the geometry of life. The stars and planets are a certain set distance away due to harmonics, the nodes of standing waves as we see on a microcosm level with the chladni plates. The Moon is exactly 400 times smaller than the Sun and exactly 400 times closer to Earth than the Sun which gives us the eclipse effect, the optical illusion that they are the same size; again a beautiful sequence of numbers. The Moon keeps the Earth at a 23.5 degree tilt acting as a planetary stabiliser and keeping water as a liquid. The number 9 is the mathematical fingerprint of God, energy into physical matter, the primal point of unity.

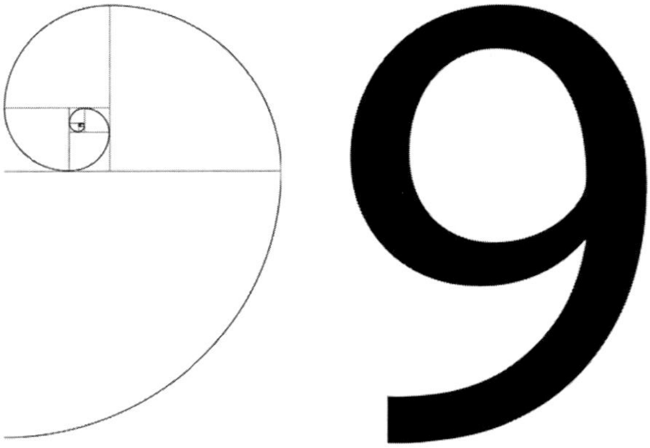

(Fig 1.0: Fibonacci Sequence and Number 9)

The sun emits photons that are conversations to our DNA. It is also a burning ball of gas that burns Hydrogen into heat and light. The Mandelbrot set, the symbol of nature's mathematical law, the chaos theory; the underlying order within natural phenomenon; is also a complex set of mathematics that will not deviate. Humans are base 10 mathematics and time for instance is base 60. Light condensed is matter, (the three stages of matter, again referring to numbers (3) are gas, liquid and solid) and then nephesh (Hebrew for living being (soul), is added to create the living being that is ourselves. Sound when its octaves are increased by 40 turn to light. We have a gigantic system of numbers and sonic equations. Light is significant when we talk of Angels too which is again something we will delve into later. The universal power is electromagnetism which is male electric combined with female magnetism, the two opposite currents, male and female, duality. Contrary to the beliefs of many the universe is a trinity not a duality or as the bible expresses it – Samson (Sun) and Delilah (Delilah derives from Dalketh, meaning 'doorway of darkness'). Duality is the effect but the cause is the singular existence. Duality is two different movements of the same event, stemming from the

'One'. We can only see less than 1% of the frequency spectra, the 7 colours or a combination of those colours. Light is an oscillation of the electromagnetic field and colour is dependent upon the frequency of that oscillation. We have a very limited bandwidth within the 3rd dimensional octave but that can all change. It is quite apparent that all this analysed there is a great mathematical mind, a creator out there, but it is not the god of religions, it, whatever it is, is far greater. Between 1989 and 1993 the COBE Experiment (Cosmic Background Explorer) which was a satellite that recorded the extremities of the universe, proved that there was once a 'One Time Beginiing' commonly known as the 'Big bang' a flash of energy so great it created all things in that instant with light staying ahead of gravity in order to reach its programmed locations. To me an abstract concept of the creator, the eureka moment, the idea manifesting into physical reality,"I think therefore I am", it is a wonderful prospect.

So to continue with the theme of DNA; Genesis, meaning 'beginning', actually refers to 'Gene/Genetics of Isis' and for those who are familiar with ancient Egypt you will recognise Isis as a goddess. Isis; however is the cosmic womb, the balance; IS-IS. The cosmic centre where stars are created is believed to be powered by Sirius A, which again has many Isis associations. This is the first book of the bible which sees Moses and Noah, again something we will talk about later in greater detail as we analyse the various biblical stories.

So what is the word? As I say there is always an astronomical and body universe aspect to these meanings. In astronomical terms when we look back at ancient belief systems the Hindu's believe that the primordial sound that created the universe was OM. Om also has a wavelength of 7.38cm which is also the distance between Human eyes and also between our nose to chin.

The Hebrew sacred scrolls were called the 'song of songs' or the Song of Solomon, song means a short metrical composition that is designed for the voice/singing; in others words a mantra/chant. Solomon is the sun in three languages, which we cover more in the religions section later. So that as a combination is really the song of the sun, vocal vibrations. In the body universe; Human DNA has 4 nucleotides, Adenine, Thymine, Guanine, and Cytosine, their letters have 64 combinations, and they are a language, an alphabet. In simple basic Gemetria; which is the numerical value of words; the number 64 is God. "In the beginning

(Fig 1.1: Hindu symbol of 'Om')

was the Word, and the Word was with God, and the Word was God"… it is talking about human DNA, the building blocks of life.

Verse 1.1

ADAM & EVE

Adam and Eve were the first people to inhabit the world; according to the bible and its divisions of the Hebrew Scriptures. Eve was created from the rib of Adam (rib, meaning to separate as one) and they lived peacefully together in the Garden of Eden (the human body, separated / nuclear fission; atoms within the body). We all come from Adam, the atom. But Eve was tempted by the serpent to eat the forbidden fruit from the tree of knowledge, good and evil.

The apple is associated with knowledge; a revelatory state; revealing something unknown. It is an allusion; a figure of speech, in which one refers covertly or indirectly to an object or circumstance from an external context. It is left to the audience to make the connection; in other words a hidden meaning; knowledge hidden from the masses but not the select few that they wish to keep to themselves; stated directly or in this case indirectly by its author in the same vein as political double speak, saying one thing but actually meaning something else, there is effectively two languages being spoken in parallel.

But did this really happen? In the physical sense no. Adam is referring again to the universal and human make-up; the atom. The creation of Eve from Adam is talking about ionic bonding, the electron being passed between atoms; the electron is a current of negative charge which is why Eve is seen as a negative influence on Adam. From Adam (atom) came the even (Eve, even number) in the form of ionic bonding. Magnetic force is a negative current. Many of the world religions devalue women and the feminine polarity and this is scientifically why. This is symbolized by head and face coverings in the many world religions, the concealment of shame. The fig leaf is also symbolic of covering shame.

On 21st September we have the equinox also known as Trees, equal day and night, and from that viewpoint you can see both light and dark, good and evil, this is the good and evil spoken about in the Adam & Eve story. This is also the time astronomically where Ophiuchus, the serpent, crosses this event; the tempting serpent is really a constellation of the celestial equator which coincides with the date of the equinox (21st September). 'Ember' as in September and other months means 'dying fire', which is when winter sets in, when the fire/sun is burning to an ember.

From the atom we get the 'Holy Trinity'. This is again the 3 component parts of the atom. The Neutron is the father, the Proton is the son and the Electron is the Holy Ghost/Spirit. When electrons become ionised and excited they give off a cloud, called an 'Electron Cloud' this bares striking similarity to a ghost, this is the Holy Ghost or Holy Spirit. A spirit is the non-decaying spin of the electron that can enter different realms by transiting between magnetic field lines. This has been recorded in recent months, and entities have been filmed travelling this way by scientists. See www.Thunderenergy.com.

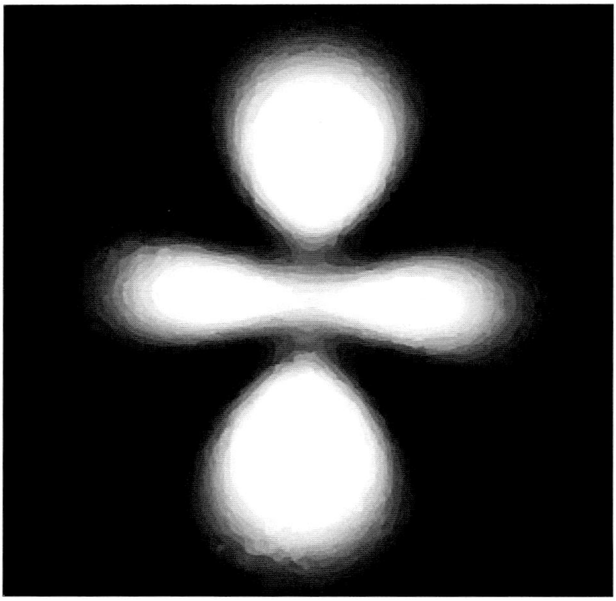

(Fig 1.2: Electron Cloud = the Holy Ghost)

Verse 1.2

THE GODS OF RELIGION ARE REALLY THE PLANETS

As we briefly indicated in the introduction religion is Astrotheology, the worship of the planets; the 7 visible planets to be more precise. So on that basis let's look at the main religions and the planet or planets that coincide with that belief system.

CHRISTIANITY:

(Fig 1.3: The symbol of Christinaity)

Christianity: We will deal with Christianity in greater detail later on when we go into the Jesus story, explaining why and what Jesus really is/was. But in essence it is Sun worship. The followers of Christianity go to Church on Sunday (Sun-Day) and their symbol; the cross refers to the Sun, again we will detail this later. The fish originates from the Genesis pattern, the geometry of life, a stage called vesica Pisces.

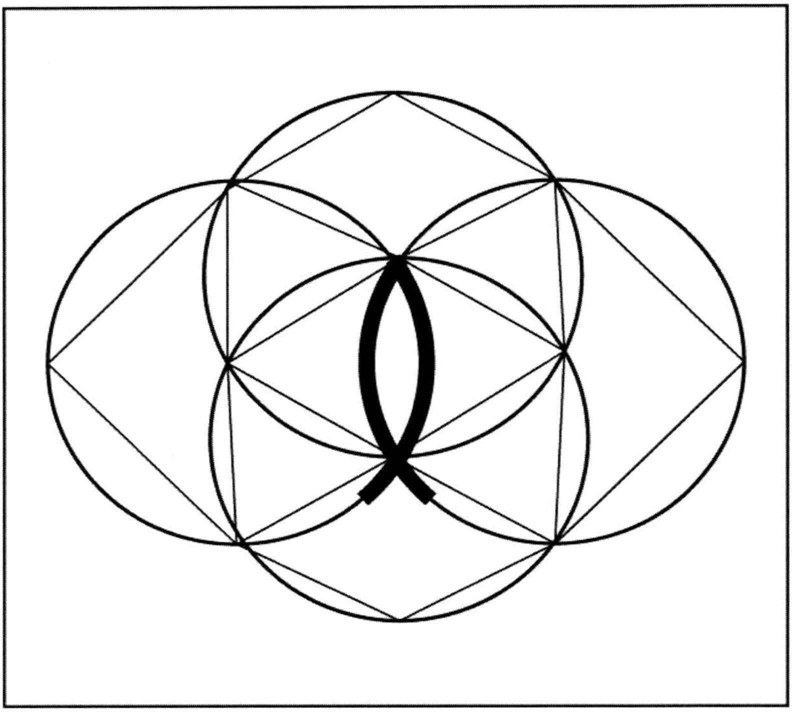

(Fig 1.4: Vesica Pisces among the latter stages of the Genesis pattern with the fish symbol)

ISLAM:

(Fig 1.5: Symbol representing the religion of Islam)

Islam: As you will see from the Islamic flag this religion is mainly the worship of the planet Venus and the Moon. Venus and the Moon are the aligning planets of the Yin, the passive feminine principle of the universe, the Electromotive force, the negative charge. When we analyse the word Allah in the Egyptian language we get AL = the and Lah = Moon, in other words the 'Moon' or Mu-On meaning negative light. This is why we can see the crescent Moon on every Mosque around the world. These planets also give answers to many practices within the religion itself such as the promise of 72 virgins. So where did this originate?

Venus orbits in a Pentagram shape and is therefore associated with the number 5, Muslims pray 5 times daily. Muslims also fast from sunset to sunrise which is the night, the realm of the Moon. At dawn they eat, they break-fast (breakfast).

(Fig 1.6: The pentagram)

The points of the pentagram touch the circle of the pentacle every 72 degrees and Venus; in zodiac astrological terms; is the sub-ruler of Virgo which in Latin means Virgin, therefore we get 72 virgins, it is celestial in origin. The promise of 72 women awaiting the brave is yet another example of religions offering rewards that are fabricated. Religion uses reward or threats and fear to control their followers, crowd control. Venus is also the star of America. At this point we will introduce another practice that this time involves the planet Saturn (from where we get the character Satan) Saturn is so influential in world events; from wedding rings and earrings, to wearing black at funerals, to global law and time; to films like Lord of the Rings and Darth Vader (dark father) in starwars; that it cannot go unmentioned. At Mecca meaning Makkah/Cube, Muslims walk around the Kaaba (black cube) 7 times anti-clockwise. Saturn's orbit is anti-clockwise and it has 7 visible rings when observed from Earth. This again has its origin from a planetary source. The black box is symbolic of Saturn (finite, Cronos-god of time/grim reaper) Saturn is also where we get the word Satan, the corruptible energy.

Allah's daughters; el-Lat, el-Uzza, and Manat ;are really the Sun, Venus and Jupiter, Halal food is Allah anagrammed …Venus and the Moon is female fertility, the Moon for obvious monthly (Moonth) reasons but Venus also due to its connection to the female genitals. The Mons Veneris (mound of Venus) and the Labia Majoris (cleft of Venus). Islam have the Hijri which is the Lunar calendar to set out their yearly calendar of worship. Females of this religion wear the Hijab which means partition/barrier being cut off in other words.

It is the Holy Grail, the womb; from where we all enter this world as spirit becomes matter and in mathematical terms we square the circle making the infinite the finite. It derives from Graal meaning vessel of God.

JUDAISM:

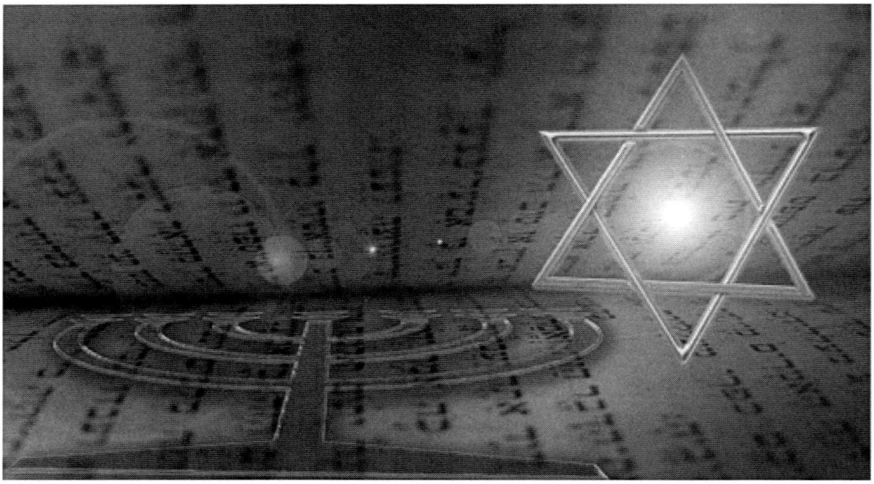

(Fig 1.7: Menorah - 7 arm candle holder from Jewish faith = the 7 visible planets)

Judaism: This religion is most influential in the world today, or at least the Zionist factions of Judaism, their religious book the Torah giving rise to the word Tarot. Or has their sacred scrolls were originally called the; 'Song of songs' or the song of Solomon, song meaning a short metrical composition, so again we are talking numbers. We get the word Jew and Judaism from Judah, and it gave rise to words such as Judge, Jury, Judiciary, as Saturn is the god of law. Saturn is a magnetic force which contracts, in law we sign contracts. Judges wear black robes which is the attire of the Saturnalian brotherhoods. So again Judaism is heavily influenced by the planet Saturn and Jews often wear a black box on their foreheads in the region of their third eye, again the symbol of Saturn. But it also has other planetary influence too. The symbol of Judaism is the seal of Solomon (or star of David) Solomon is really the Sun in three languages, Sol – Om – On. Sol (Latin) Om (Hindu) and On (Coptic Egyptian, Coptic meaning Christian). Saturn is the black Sun. Saturday (Saturn's day) used to also be the original Sabbath, or black Sabbath for the Ozzy Osbourne rock fans out there.

This seal is the 4 elements sealed by the fifth element, the ether, the male aspect of the Yesod, the higher substance of light (Sun). Again this all fits in later when we discuss Jesus. The Judaic faith is also highly influenced by Yahweh, which in Tetragrammaton is YHWH, this is the 4 elements, Yod-He-Wau-He. Jehovah or JHVH is the Latin equivalent (or in modern internet search engine, Yahu or as we know it; Yahoo). Yehweh and the 4 elements also play a major role in the 4 gospels which is covered later. Even the current Israeli Prime minister Benjamin (favourite son) Netanyahu (Hebrew: וּהָיְנַתְנ, "God has given"- Yahu = Yehweh) has these connotations.

The Jewish skull cap is the ring of Saturn and also the Royal wave indicates this too, symbolic of the giant rings. Even Remembrance Day parades that we are told are to commemorate the fallen, the war dead is not what it seems. Saturn rules the winter, Capricorn (Capricornus – Horned Goat) and is associated with the Red & Black poppy, also significant on Remembrance Day parades. The poppies are laid out as a circular wreath (rings of Saturn). Remembrance also has another hidden meaning, which is token/souvenir; the aristocracies are in their belief system harnessing the energy of sacrifice which they believe enhances their own power; as they take the energy of their victims. When we have an election to vote a new leader, the word EL originally meant Saturn and the black ballot box is yet another Saturn symbol, EL later came to mean God .

Keeping with the theme of Royalty, the British Royal family believe themselves to be from the Royal house of David, again Jewish/Judaic references. The tribe of Judah (Judah meaning young Lion-Sun symbol) were influenced by the Chaldeans who ruled Babylon for a short time. Chaldean derives from Ur Chur which means Moon worshippers. So when we get a Monarchy or

Monarch we are really saying 'Moon Arch'. So with the Sun and Moon we have the two great luminaries, the realms of day and night and from that we get the two religions of Christianity (Sun) and Islam (Moon).

Keeping with the theme of Royalty and Judaic influence, Jacob, of Judaic faith, was visited by god whilst upon his pillow (Jacob's pillow) and was told that his seed would spread across the world to rule as Kings and Queens until the return of the Promised land, Israel (Jacobs pillow is also known as the 'Coronation Stone' upon which Royalty are coronated). In the UK our flag is the Union Jack, which is the Union of Jacob and as British we are saying that we are a 'Man of the contract' B'rith (covenant/contract) ish (man) and Britain is land of the contract; that contract is with the Hebrew god. The Red, White and Blue is Egyptian but the crosses on the Union Jack are the Quarter days and cross quarter days; which are the 8 Sun festivals.

Israel is: *Is* (Isis-Moon), *Ra* (Egyptian Sun god), *El* (Saturn)... A combination of a celestial theme. Israel is also called the land of milk and honey, which is the pineal gland secretion (secret), which will be covered in the section about medical astronomy. American Presidents and even British Prime Ministers swear allegiance to Israel as they take office, they are put into these positions of power by the Zionist shadow people, who influence every significant aspect of society (Zion = synonym for Jerusalem). In the UK Prime Ministers; such as Tony Blair, are members of a group called "Friends of Israel". The UK also had a major part to play with the creation of the state of Israel with the Balfour Declaration (see Fig 1.9).

(Fig 1.8: Here we see President Bush in his skull cap at the Wailing Wall in Jerusalem. The Wailing Wall is so-called as it is meant to be the remnants of the Temple of Solomon and many cry out loud, or wail, in sorrow)

Foreign Office,
November 2nd, 1917.

Dear Lord Rothschild,

I have much pleasure in conveying to you, on behalf of His Majesty's Government, the following declaration of sympathy with Jewish Zionist aspirations which has been submitted to, and approved by, the Cabinet

"His Majesty's Government view with favour the establishment in Palestine of a national home for the Jewish people, and will use their best endeavours to facilitate the achievement of this object, it being clearly understood that nothing shall be done which may prejudice the civil and religious rights of existing non-Jewish communities in Palestine, or the rights and political status enjoyed by Jews in any other country"

I should be grateful if you would bring this declaration to the knowledge of the Zionist Federation.

Yours

Arthur James Balfour

(Fig 1.9: Arthur Balfour, Former British Foreign Secretary)

The world of religion is gripped by sin. Sin is really the Hebrew 'schin', (the symbol was made famous by Mr Spock in Star trek), which is again the yesod. In male terms it is light, the Sun, in female terms the yesod is fertility Moon based. When we place the letters of schin, SC within YHWH we get Yeshua. The cross with Jesus is really the 4 elements plus the sun. But as we say we will go into that detail later. Suffice to say Sin is another method of control by fear it does not exist and neither does Hell which has ancient Egyptian connotations, which we will explain in the section that deals with ancient Egypt.

When Jews engage in the vile practice of circumcision, (and I am attacking the practice, not the faith), they are carrying out a ritual to appease the Dark Moon, Lilith, the 'lunar apogee'. Lilith has dominion over children for the first 8 days of their lives and it is no coincidence that this practice is carried out on the child's 8th day of incarnation.

Overleaf, Figure 2.0 depicts the black box of Kaaba in Mecca, where Muslims pilgrim. Figure 2.1 then also depicts a man of Jewish faith with a black box over his third eye. Two identical symbols yet two opposing and often warring religions, yet unknowingly at the level of the masses doing the exact same thing.

Fig 2.0: The black box of Saturn in Mecca)

(Fig 2.1: The cube worn by Jewish Rabbi)

Is it so obvious that they can't see it, hidden in plain sight? The black box is not only a symbol of the planet Saturn but it is also anything with an input and output such as the human brain. All religions are doing just that, the same thing, worshipping the same planets under different identities, those being the individual Gods given to them by a controlling and ruling elite.

CATHOLISM:

(Fig 2.2: Catholic Priest during 'Holy Communion')

Catholic: Catholic means 'universal' and it is no surprise then that they too worship the seven visible planets. In many Catholic schools children are separated into planets rather than classes, for example the Sun class, Moon class and Jupiter class, based around these 7 visible planets. This belief system is conducted from the Vatican which derives from Vatika, the pineal gland, the third eye. The pineal gland is a pine and this is why at such places as the Vatican they have statues of a pine. It is also where we get the phrase pea brain. They are foretellers of the future by means of understanding the celestial narrative; the zodiac. The Christian festival of Epiphany which is a Christian feast celebrating the manifestation of the divine nature of Jesus to the Gentiles; is really referring to the Pineal gland which is also known as epiphysis cerebri.

(Fig 2.3: Pine cone = Pineal gland, as seen here at the Vatican)

Rome was formerly called Saturnalia which again is reference to the planet Saturn. When the Roman Empire ruled England it did so from a city called York. The Roman church now controls America from the New York, which sees such locations as 'Time Square'. Time and squares are both symbols of the planet Saturn. They also changed the first month of the year from March to January.

In the catholic church we have Nuns, which in Egyptian means the pre-creational waters and they are often called Sisters which derives from Isis-star (Moon or sometimes Sirius A) a mother superior. Isis is the cosmic womb symbolised by the Dove which is nurturing and perfect motherhood, magna mater, Great mother, from where we get words such as material, matter and mater. Isis and her Son/Sun Horus were the original Mary and Jesus.

(Fig 2.4 & 2.5: The two different types of arches indicating Sun & Moon cults, Sun arch (left) of Roman origin, 'Sol Invictus' and the 4 gates of the vagina (Moon fertility cults) on the right)

This is significant in the title Arch Deacon, arch & Deccan are both Sun references. In the Catholic religion we also have Monks who worship in the Monastery, this word again means Moon-star. The Vatican also controls Maritime Law, the Uniform Commerce Code, in other words global business. They control many things as a result of the Donation of Constantine. Pinnacle to this commerce code is the business water channel the Suez Canal, or Suez backwards is Zeus; the mythical God of Olympus (Zeus is really the Planet Jupiter). Planetary references are everywhere to be seen and found. Jupiter has violent storms and is symbolised with the lightning bolt, the destructive weapon of Zeus. And this is why many of our pop stars and alike have the lightning bolt across their faces.

In the 1500's the Roman Catholic church, which is in itself a fake Christian front, created what is known as the Cestie Que Vie trust, in effect placing the whole planet in their control by means of that trust, by a 'Right of Claim' never challenged. It is symbolised by the 'Papal Tiara' the 3 tiered Crown (Vatican Crown). It controls Maritime law which is the law of the land and sea and claims ownership (Ship = a sea/water reference) of all persons, property and salt of the Earth. Even the United States of America is really a corporation acting under Lex Fori (Law of the Forum - which is Roman Law) under the Potus (President) acting as 'Vassal King' (holder of land) answerable to the British Monarchy who are themselves answerable to the Vatican. The President operates with a senate (Roman system) on Capitol Hill (Rome = Capitoline Hill) both also have the Sun symbol of the Eagle. The Pope's title is Vicarius Filii Dei which means 'In Place Of The Son Of God'. When this word is written in Roman numerals with the introduction of gemetria, the numerical value of letters, we get 666, the Pope in other words is the Anti-Christ. "Jesus cast 7 demons out of her" Rome is built upon 7 hills.

The Vatican created 3 trusts, (1) (Unum Sanctum- Crown of the land) When a child is born he/she loses all benefits/entitlements and rights to land upon birth. (2) (Aeterni Regis – Eternal Crown) When a child is born, in a delivery room (delivery = to exchange goods), their birth certificate (Berth = allocated docking place) is sold as a bond (legally enforceable) to the private central bank of the nation of birth and they therefore lose all right to their flesh condemning them to perpetual servitude as a slave. In court when we are prosecuted this comes from pros-se cutis which means to represent your own skin, we are all convicts, the victim of a con which is the legal system (3) When a child is Baptised parents are handing over the child's soul to the Vatican therefore removing the child's right over their own soul and denying them the right to stand as a person only a creature/thing without soul (Lost at sea) which is called 'Gift of Title of the soul' the 'Baptismal Certificate' which is then held in the Vatican vaults.

The whole legal system is enforcing these trusts and our courts are enforcing Ecclesiastical/Cannon law as they did in the Spanish Inquisition, this also refers to both Maritime law (in court we have the Bench which derives from Bank) and also Astronomy but that's for another day. The Vatican bank is run by Zionist Jews and it is their religious duty to charge the Goyim as much interest as possible on the likes of loans. The world and its systems are not as they seem The Vatican is run behind the scenes by the Jesuit Order and the 'Black Pope' and they are Crypto-Jews with world dominaton at the helm of their ship.

Here is a quote from Ex- Prime Minister of Israel Menechem Begin "*Our race is the Master race. We are divine Gods on this planet. We are as different from the inferior races as they are from insects. Other races are beasts and animals, cattle at best. Our destiny is to rule over the inferior races. The masses will lick our feet and serve us as our slaves".*

They want a one world system with Jerusalem as a global capital.

JEHOVAH'S WITNESSES:

"Freemasonry is a Jewish establishment" - Rabbi Isaac Wise.

(Fig 2.6: Charles Taze Russell)

We mustn't forget also the likes of Jehovah's Witnesses and Mormons. The Jehovah's witnesses were created by Charles Taze Russell who was a high degree Mason involved in B'nai B'rith, the covenant, a Judaic group, the masonic brotherhoods. And if you look at his tombstone in America (Pittsburgh) you will see a multitude of Masonic/ Egyptian symbology, Egypt being the focus of the Scottish Rites of freemasonry. The ancient Pharisees as mentioned on the back cover were an ancient Jewish sect (group of people with different religious beliefs) who believe that they had a higher sanctity than anyone else, that they were more sacred and holy. For those who are familiar with such agendas as the New World Order (NWO), that belief will be instantly recognisable as a Zionist theology too, this is of course because it is a continuation of the same sect.

(Fig 2.7: Charles Taze Russell's Grave)

When Jehovah's witnesses knock on your door they are doing what they describe 'The work' this is again a freemasonic term, but they say 'The great work'. Jehovah is really the 4 elements, the Latin equivalent of the Hebrew Yahweh. JHVH and YHWH. The watchtower, the magazine of the Jehovah's witnesses is referring to the guardians of the 4 cardinal points, north, east, south and west; or in Egypt this is the 4 sons of Horus. It is their belief that the battle of Armageddon is the final days when all who are not of this faith will perish. But Armageddon or the nearby Mount (Har) Megiddo probably gave its name to Armageddon and has seen many ancient battles, battle of Har-Megiddo or Megeddo under the leaderhsip of a Hebrew by the name of

Barrack, strange considering the current but outgoing president of the USA shares the same name. Anyway, they'll most likely be waiting a long time for their version. They state that following Armageddon there will be a 1000 years of paradise on Earth. This is of course unknowlingly refering to a 1000 years of the 'New World Order' a one world system of rule under the energies of the planet Saturn.

Megiddo is in northern Israel near Kibbutz Megiddo, about 30 km south-east of Haifa, known for its historical, geographical, and theological importance, especially under its Greek name Armageddon. Megiddo is strategically located at the head of a pass through the Carmel Ridge overlooking the Jezreel Valley from the west. It is strategical as is the Suez Canal today; Suez is Zeus in reverse, the planet Jupiter.

(Fig 2.8: Joseph Smith)

MORMONISM:

The Mormons were also created by a high degree mason, Joseph Smith and Mormon comes from Mormo, the god of the living dead. All is not as it seems.

There are of course many other religions such as Hinduism who believe that the primordial sound that created the universe was Om. As was stated Om is a name for the Sun in their language and as we discussed in the Judaic section above the word Solomon is the sun in three languages and their sacred scrolls the song of songs or song of Solomon is relevant here too with that in mind. They also have the new age version of Jesus which is Sananda, this in Sanskrit means aspect of Lakshmi, the female aspect of the Sun, who is associated with abundance, this is the wealth of knowledge from the Sun.

I think it's worth bearing in mind that Religions preace peace for all yet the Vatican is the largest share holder of Berreta, the Chruch of England has £10 million shares in General Electric (GE) and the Jehovah's witnesses (Watchtower Society) have a 50% share stake in Rand Cam, these three companies all deal in the arms trade.

But for now we will stay with the main religions as a base from which to continue.

Verse 1.3

FESTIVALS

The festivals that people the world over engage in also have astronomical significance. For example Mother's day, which comes from magna mater, or great mother, is referring to the Egyptian goddess Isis and Father's day, which is held on 21st June which is the summer solstice and is therefore Sun worship. On Pancake Day we make pancakes which are symbolic of the Sun and it is held before lent, which means lengthening, in other words the Sun coming into its power, the summer, lengthening of the day/light. Pancake Day is known as Shrove Tuesday which derives from the word shrive meaning penance, the Sun paying penance for its disappearance, namely the winter months which sees man and crops suffer and die each year. In the month of May we see another such festival were we have the practice of Morris dancing, dancing around the May pole - a phallic symbol and symbol of male power. The British Union Jack flag is also symbolic of the 8 festivals of the Sun, the solstices and quarter days and cross quarter days making the crosses of the symbol itself. Christmas is the biggest Sun festival of all with Easter following behind it, both refer to the Solar Sun which i have mentioned in more detail in other chapters. When we watch stars (astronomical reference) at awards events such as the 'Golden Globe' awards and even the oscars we are witnessing Sun symbology too.

Astronomical symbology is everywhere in our society and there are further examples later on in the brands and logos verse. There isn't necessarily a problem with Sun or planetary worship so long as that form of worship does no harm of any kind to others. This is just highlighting the hidden languages of this matter that most never see or contemplate.

Verse 1.4

EGYPT - THE LAND OF MYSTERY

There are many ancient cultures of great knowledge and understanding, such as Babylon and Sumeria, which is the modern day Iraq. For those who are familiar with author Zecharia Sitchin you will be aware that he translated and gave the world many books following his interpretation of the Sumerian scrolls.

(Fig 2.9: The late Zecharia Sitchin)

But in the same vein that religious books like the bible are a mistruth this is my belief of Sitchin's translation which is giving a physical story but yet actually referring to a deeper esoteric reality. Before we move onto Egypt let's analyse Sitchin's work. Sitchin mentioned planet X, Nibiru, it is no coincidence that the Egyptian name of the planet Venus is Neb-Heru. Many people the world over are seeing a planet like object next to the Sun and claim that this is planet X. There are two natural explanations for this, they are natural phenomena. Firstly Sundogs, their official name Perihelion, which occurs when the sun is on the horizon; the sun's light shining off ice particles in the atmosphere. Secondly we have a natural phenomenon called Hunters Moon which occurs when the Moon is setting and the Sun is rising, and because the Moon is a reflection of Sunlight it looks like two Suns in the sky at the same time. Sitchin also goes into the Anunnaki and Anu. Anu is the ultimate physical universal atom of creation, it is the centre of the two joining rings of the figure 8 (infinity). He also details two characters called Enki and Enlil, the snake brothers. This is the double helix of human DNA shaped like two snakes coiled together. The Enki and Enlil story and the battles between them; are the two opposing hemispheres of the brain, left and right. Anunnaki means to change the atom for the better, maybe this is referring to genetic tinkering, an upgrade of some kind? The Lord's Prayer are the 'Maxims of Anu' (Maxim = a short statement of a principle rule or conduct).

Even this has a surface level and also a much deeper level if you look deep enough.

Egypt is a land of intrigue, the ancient Egyptian race were advanced beyond their years and even beyond ours with their monuments and their knowledge base. They knew the frequency of DNA, they knew the Fibonacci code thousands of years before modern science, they knew the speed of light thousands of years before Einstein theorised it. When we look at the pyramids we see advanced building techniques and secret knowledge that we still cannot decipher in the 21st century.

And most astonising is that there is a planetary and solar system pyramid matrix system whereby famous monuments refer to each other in their mathematical sizing and locations. On Earth we have famous monuments put there, or so we believe, by the ancients who knew many secrets to the make up of the cosmos and they used advanced mathematics to conceal coordinates of other monuments within the numerology of their own monuments and this extends to the planet Mars. Was this a GPS homing system for those from other worldly locations, a guidance system for them to find certain places?

So let's analyse the mathematics between monuments and societies that we are taught were primitve. We use Greenwich in London as our time meridian, this is incorrect, the real Meridian is the Great Pyramid in Giza, the exact centre of all landmass of Earth. These monuments are all connected by Grid-Vectors from Mexico and Peru, to England and Egypt and beyond that too.

Stonehenge in Wiltshire, UK, is a 360 degree circle that has 60 outer stones and 15 centre blocks. When we use the mathematical formula 360 x 60 it equals 21,600 which is a multiple of 51 degrees divided by 10 divided by 42.35 (51 degrees + 10 minutes + 42,35 seconds) this is the exact location of Stonehenge. 2160 is also in years the age of the zodiac sign transition, each sign rules for that period of time.

Stonehenge is 288 ft across which when multiplied by PI and multiplied by 15 (centre block number) divided by the square root 15 we get 52,562 which is the exact grid longitude of Stonehenge. 52,562 divided by 360 PI = a square root of 2160. Square root 2160 divided by 2 PI = the grid reference of the 3 smaller Pyramids in Egypt (adjacent to the Great Pyramid et al) which equals the square root 2.71 which is the megalithic yard (2.72). 360 divided by the Megalithic yard squared = the radius of the Great Pyramid itself.

When we use the 3 dimensional formation of the Great Pyramid using double PI we get 9929.184896 which is the encoded grid latitude of the Pyramid of Cydonian City on Planet Mars. And in addition to this the famous face on Mars has a grid latitude of 4523.893421 which when divided by the square root 2160 equals 97.3386882 which is the diameter of Stonehenge. The Cydonian city is also an exact map overlay of Avebury in Wiltshire, UK. This correlation between encoded mathematical co-ordinates also extends to other Pyramids too such as in Mexico and elsewhere as well as other monuments/ sacred locations around the globe. We have a complex yet beautiful system of coded mathematics of the advanced level that we arrogantly believe is patented by modern science; we are very much wrong.

It's time to put down our school text books and learn the truth...

All American Presidents, bar one, are related to the Pharaoh's of Egypt and all are also related to European Royalty including the British Royal house. The current British Prime Minster David Cameron (Minster = Moon-star) is related to the current Queen, Boris Johnson the former London mayor and George Osbourne, the current British chancellor are all related to him and Royalty too. It has been a bloodline of rule for many thousands of years. They continue the philosophy of self-aggrandisement, using knowledge to enhance their own power and influence. This is the language of the initiates from the

Egyptian mystery schools to the modern day masonic halls. As former US president Roosevelt once said "Presidents are selected, not elected" and in the words of Stalin "It's not who votes that counts, it's who counts the votes", the whole system is rigged in the favour of the bloodlines, the elites, el-ite, meaning god's chosen ones.

They used hieroglyphs which were a secret coded language and they were responsible for the many things we do in the modern day. Egyptian systems go to the very heart of British government even today. The houses of parliament have a tower called Big Ben, which is the benbenet, the pyramid capstone. The river Thames was formerly called Isis, the Egyptian river goddess. Even Royalty and its incestuous relationships stems from ancient Egypt. Its influence has stood the test of time.

Even good old British pubs are sometimes named after Egyptian subjects, such as the Red Lion, which is the symbol of the Pharaohs of lower Egypt (Northern Egypt).

Egypt originally wrought the matriarchal system of female balance and this led to Moon cults and alike, Isis was associated with Sirius A but when the new Moon appeared it was seen as the cosmic appearance of Isis too. This raised the waters of the Nile (Ye-or meaning to shine/Year) which fertilised the crops and gave rise to a celebration called ' Argha Noah', and this is of course reminiscent of flood waters and Argha Noah = Noah's Ark, there is of course a bodily version too which we will cover when we discuss Noah in more detail later on. Isis and Horus was the original Mary and Jesus as Sirius A was believed to have created our Sun.

(Fig 3.0: Isis and Horus)

Place names are significant too, Paris taken from Parisi meaning temple of Isis and Switzerland meaning sisters of Isis.

Later in Egypt's history the matriarchal system was overpowered by the Patriarchal male system forced by the priests of Aten and it became a Sun male power based society. The Aten/Amun RA (from where we get amen) priests travelled enforcing this new system placing Obelisks to mark their territory (Egyptian – Gyptian = Gypsy/traveller). They introduced Sun worship or as originally translated War-ship, the male dominance. The Sun comes into power from March onwards and that's what an army does, it marches.

One such place was the place we know as Palestine or in the German pronunciation, Germanic being the origins of English, Palla-stein meaning concrete obelisk. The obelisk is a phallic symbol of male authority. Obelisks can be seen at symbolic places today such as the Vatican, Washington DC and the City of London. This is also true of church spires which are also phallic symbols, what do you aspire to be, same meaning? Even children's nursery rhymes have a sun worshipping theme, such as these lyrics from the nursery rhyme the 'Hokey Cokey'; *"Knees bent, arms stretched, rah, rah, rah"!* This is telling you to bow down and worship the sun god Ra (Rah).

(Fig 3.1: Obelisks fascination! (Left) - The City of London, (Center) - Washington DC and (Right) - The Vatican)

In relation to the story of the obelisk - Isis was the wife and sister of Osiris (we get the word sister from Isis-star) and after Osiris was murdered by his brother set, he was chopped into 14 pieces. This is Moon based which has 28 astronomical houses, 14 at the top and 14 below. Isis found 13 pieces but could not find the 14th, Osiris's penis and therefore an obelisk meaning Baal's shaft; replaced it and it has been a symbol globally ever since. Osiris is important to Royalty also. When a person is knighted before the Queen (isis, meaning she of the throne) they become entitled Sir, this word emanated from O(sir)is.

Sun worship is Egyptian in origin. The Sun was split into 4 parts, at dawn the Sun is Horus, where we get the word Horizon which means Horus-risen, it is also where we get the concept of our time, where is the Horus/Sun now? Horus means 'hour' and in hieroglyphs Horus is depicted as HR, which is the abbreviation for hour. There is also a word 'orison' which means to speak/

pray to a deity, and the word pray contains the word 'Ra'. At 12 noon, the most high/zenith, the Sun is RA from where we get modern words such as 'ra-diation' and 'ra-diance', to give off heat, like the Sun does, (Right Ascension, a series of astrological coordinates used to locate the positions of celestial bodies). Sunset is Set and Osiris is the Sun beneath your feet, which is why Osiris is the god of the underworld, Hell, or Helios which is the Sun; there is no such place as the biblical hell, that is a fear based control system, burn in Hell, burn in Helios, the Sun is a ball of fire. Set, Djeudje, where we get the name George, battles with Apophis, the dragon as the Sun disappears. This is the origin of George and the Dragon. The English flag, Red & White is lower and Upper Egypt merged. There is so much we do today that originates in Egypt. The Egyptians have no word for death only Westing which relates to the Sunset, when it disappears to travel the duat accompanied by the Akeru, the two Lion guards of the gates of the day and night.

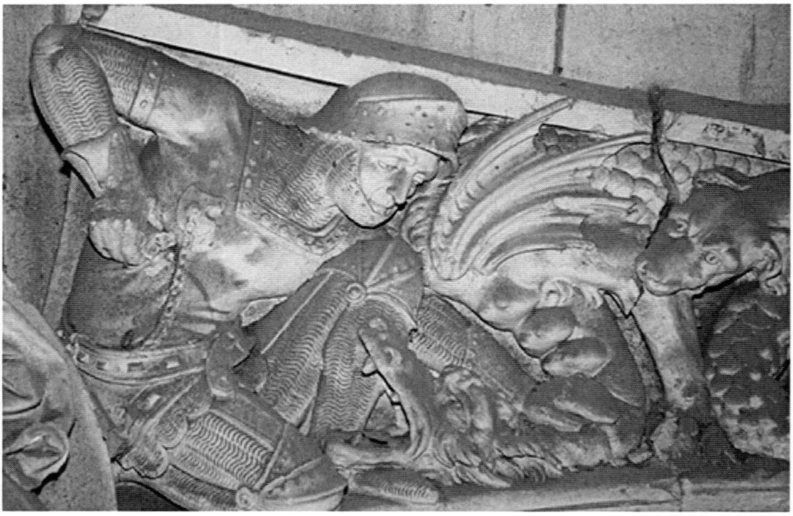

(Fig 3.2: George (Djeudje/Set) and the Dragon (Apophis)

And of course the Egyptians built or at least we believe that they built the Pyramids, pyramid means 'fire in the middle' which is the Sun in our solar system. The pyramid shape, the tetrahedron is also the symbol of fire in the platonic solids, the 3 dimensional shapes of our realm. The pyramids were not burial tombs for the Pharaoh's (Pharaoh meaning Great House-Zodiac term) they were a recreation of the electromagnetic universe, a vortex in and vortex out, for the manifestation of entities entering and leaving the 3D space, they were resonance chambers, which is how the large bricks were lifted, they were a gigantic power station harnessing Earth's energy and finely tuning it to a higher octave, they were the power point, the central network of Earth's energy leylines; since the Great pyramid is the exact centre of Earth's land mass; chanting and singing etc enhances the energy further. They were many things, but they were not what the mainstream tells us they were. The sphinx, the head of a women and the body of a Lion; is the beginning and end of the celestial narrative, Virgo to Leo in the zodiac. The sphinx is also a protector of sacred places but also of secret knowledge. The Sun and the surrounding planets are a microcosm version of the atomic structure.

Secret information is encoded for all to see and decipher, it was Thoth who in many circles was attributed as being the builder of the Pyramid. Thoth simply means thought, the right brain.

(Fig 3.3: The Abydos helicopter. Heli is Helios (sun) and copter is Coptic = Christian Egyptian)

The above image is of the Abydos helicopter in Egyptian hieroglyphs. In the same vein that Eagles were seen as Sun symbols due to their high flight, maybe this is the meaning of the ancient Helicopter in one of the oldest Egyptian temples. Just how a society who were are seen as slaves using the most basic of tools could draw a modern day mode of transport is open to suggestion. Just think how difficult it is to draw something so accurate when you haven't seen it. They must have seen them and they must have been like they are today, airborne.

The Sun plays an integral part in our past and the current modern day, we see it in many logos, brand names and in our architecture, it is the life giver and the focal point of worship for the masses, the overwhelming majority don't even know it and they have been worshipping the Sun under different identities for thousands of years, even today, and Sunday this week and next and every Sunday until the end of time. Egypt and Isis are significant in today's America too. The Egyptians used to sacrifice dogs in July/August to appease the heat from the Sun that was believed to emanate from Sirius A (Horus and Jesus, Sun & Sirius A-Isis) Today this is symbolised by the Hotdog, the iconic American way. Also on 4th July Sirius A is furthest away from our own Sun and out of sight. The founding fathers wished to commemorate this therefore that's when the American independence was signed (4th July). It was signed in Philadelphia, Philae is where the Temple of Isis stood in Egypt and Delphos is the womb, Isis is the cosmic womb/mother. On August 7, 1880 at precisely 10:59am the cornerstone of the Washington Monument obelisk was laid just as the Sun passed over Sirius. The Sun and Sirius are in a binary which is also the Kachina Hopi philosophy of premonition and prediction involving Blue and Red planets, this is the outward and inward transit of Sirius within this binary orbit with the solar Sun. And of course you have the Pyramid on the US Dollar (Dollar = dolas = deception) but that connotation is for another time as it has wider implications. The significance is present in many other hidden ways too:

(Fig 3.4: Isis in the American Dollar symbol)

Continuing with the theme of the Sun, that leads us nicely onto the 'Greatest Story Ever Told' - Jesus; Who or *what* was/is he?

You are now about to find out!

Verse 1.5

THE SECRET OF CHRIST

Imagine ancient man struggling for survival on planet Earth, the dark of night looms, a time when he was vulnerable, open to be hunted by larger carnivores, unable to effectively see his surroundings; Seeking shelter and warmth and protection. Then after he spotted the planet Venus he had the promise of the Sun, it comes second, it is the second coming! (of Christ).

Now the world is lit, man can see; the Sun is the saviour, it says "I am the light of the world", "Because of me man shall live forever" (Jesus quotes). The Sun in Hebrew is called Yes/Jes which is where we get the names Yeshua and Jesus. When we nod our heads and say yes we are symbolising Sun rise and Sun set. In ancient days the word Son and Sun were the same word; separated by early Christians to create a division to hide the true nature and meaning of this golden globe in the sky.

Psalm 84:11 (King James Version): *11 For the LORD God is a sun and shield.*

When Earth's poles push together they create a magnetic field aided by the convection of the liquid of Earth's core, the dynamo effect. This together prevents the sun's harmful rays frying the planet. This is the shield referred to in this bible passage.

The Sun activates our pineal glands (third eye) giving us wisdom beyond our realm, which is what Jesus did in the bible with his sermons to the masses.

Jesus is a metaphor for the solar sun and the life of Jesus is the Sun's transit through the 12 signs of the zodiac or in biblical terminology the 12 disciples.

The facial features of Jesus Christ are iconic and instantly recognisable throughout the world. But in a time when there were no cameras and no photographing facilities how could we know what someone of the ancient past looked like, especially when the bible and the description came hundreds of years after the event? It is far more likely that intervention took place and sabotaged the iconic image for the own means and agenda of the author or authors. It is believed in many circles that the image of Jesus given to us for many thousands of years was in fact Cesare Borgia, the son of Pope Alexander VI:

(Fig 3.5: Cesare Borgia, a striking resemblance)

And so the story begins:

The angel of the lord came down and told the Virgin Mary that she was to have the son of god, an immaculate conception, she had been chosen for this task much to the dismay of her husband Joseph. Virgo, the Latin for virgin, a zodiac constellation, appears in the sky optically rising out of the sea, 'the mare', and there we have the Virgo Mare, or the Virgin Mary. She was not a physical character but let's go with the story for now.

The planet Mercury is never more than 28 degrees from the Sun; it has the fastest orbit and is known as the messenger, this is the angel of the lord spoken about in the bible. Incidentally the clock is based on the Sun (Hour) the Moon (Minutes) and Mercury (seconds).

She travelled on a donkey with her husband seeking a place to have her child but the inn was full, the mind was full, therefore the Christ had no place to reside with so much mental activity going on, which is an esoteric message for us all to clear the mind and make way for our own Christ; the Christ consciousness.

They were allowed solace in the manger and settled to give birth to the most famous living being the Earth has ever seen. News travelled far and 3 wise men followed the Star of Bethlehem; baring gifts; which was to lead them to the Christ King.

What the bible fails to mention is that the names of these 3 wise men are really Mintaka; Alnilam and Alnitak and they are the stars of the belt of Orion (the 3 kings) following Sirius A which is the Star of Bethlehem.

(Fig 3.6: Astrononmical 'Nativity Story'; the three wise men following the star of Bethlehem)

What is also deliberately omitted is that in the constellation of Cancer we have a cluster of stars called the Manger and also 2 stars called Asellus Borealis (North Donkey)and Asellus Australis (South Donkey). Asellus means Donkey, this is the nativity story acted and played out by children in front of adoring family and friends each year; it is again astronomical in origin. Jesus was born in the manger between a Horse and Goat, this is of course Sagittarius and Capricorn (Capricornus the Horned Goat) the two Zodiac signs of November, December, January and February that surround the 25th December, which is in between them. This is also significant later on in the life of Jesus with this scripture: *"When they had come near Jerusalem and had reached Bethphage, at the Mount of Olives, Jesus sent two disciples, saying to them, 'Go into the village ahead of you, and immediately you will find a donkey tied, and a colt with her; untie them and bring them to me. If anyone says anything to you, just say this, "The Lord needs them." And he will send them immediately.'* This took place to fulfil what had been spoken through the prophet, saying, *'Tell the daughter of Zion, Look your king is coming to you, humble, and mounted on a donkey, and on a colt, the foal of a donkey.'* The disciples went and did as Jesus had directed them; they brought the donkey and the colt, and put their clothes on them, and he sat on them" [Matthew 21:1-7) These are the two donkey's referred to in this story also.

As previously stated, there is usually a medical astronomical version of the astronomical version too as both are connected. The medical astronomy to this story is that the 3 wise men of the body are the Pituitary gland, the Pineal gland and the Thalamus the 3 component parts of the third eye, and as we see in Egyptian hieroglyphs the Star of Bethlehem is a flower (Bach remedy) an aromatherapy that activates the senses of the brain including the amygdala (Mary Magdalene) into cosmic connection.

The Virgin Mary, according to Catholicism, ascended on 15th August, again this is merely the Sun moving into the constellation of Virgo and drowning it out by the brightness of its light making it seemingly disappear. It is called the 'assumption of the virgin'. Jesus began the work of his father aged 12, this is when the Sun is at its most high (12 noon) and he wondered the plains of Nazareth (meaning Priest-Kings, it never actually existed in the times of Jesus) carrying out miracles like feeding the 5000 with 5 loaves and 2 fishes. He existed and spent his last days in Jerusalem a name deriving from Urusalimum or Ursalimmu meaning 'Foundation of Shalem or Salem' who was the Canaanite god of dusk, Sunset. But again how could this happen? Well in the physical sense it didn't, again we need only look at the sky. In the zodiac Virgo, the house of bread, the 5th house of the zodiac; is the zodiac opposite of Pisces, the 2 fishes and there you have it, the 5 loaves and 2 fishes is a zodiac reference. Jesus was a carpenter and carpenters built houses, this is yet another reference to the Zodiac.

Jesus was documented as walking on water, he was the son of god, and so this was assumingly easy for him albeit a physical vessel like the rest of us. He was able to turn water into wine and cure the blind, all eyes shall see him. Again let's analyse these superhuman events putting them into an astronomical and natural context. Fig 3.7 shows the Sun/Son/Jesus walking on water, it is merely a reflection of the Sun's light bouncing off the surface of the water, not a physical man stepping over the water molecules and walking over the waves.

(Fig 3.7: Jesus walking on water)

The Sun gives the energy for water cycles and water then ferments the vineyards turning water into wine. Also, when we drink water it gets absorbed into our blood, wine is symbolic of blood as we see in holy communion festivals and alike, water is therefore turned into wine within our body as a result of our natural bodily functions and processes. He cures the blind and all eyes shall see him. This is not necessarily talking about the two physical eyes, it is talking about the third eye, the eye able to see beyond the physical world, the pineal gland (eye of Horus) and this gland is activated by the Sun, the wisdom of its light cures the blindness or in other words ignorance. The crown of thorns worn by Jesus is referring to the Sun's corona.

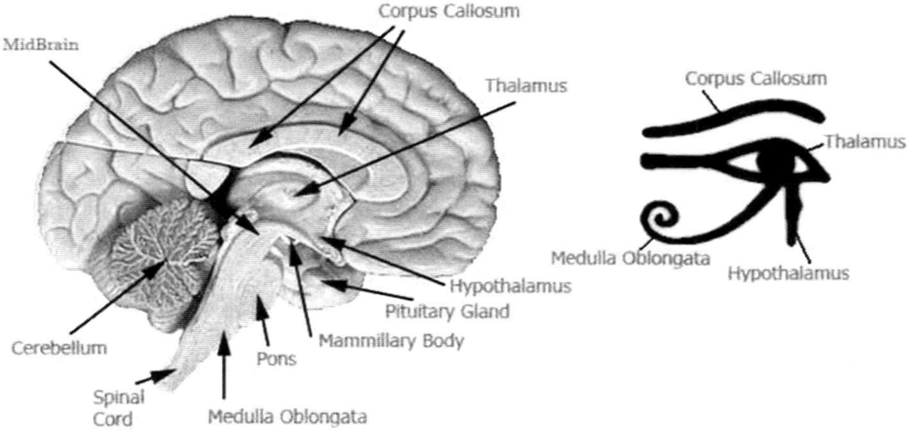

(Fig 3.8: Pineal Gland and the eye of Horus)

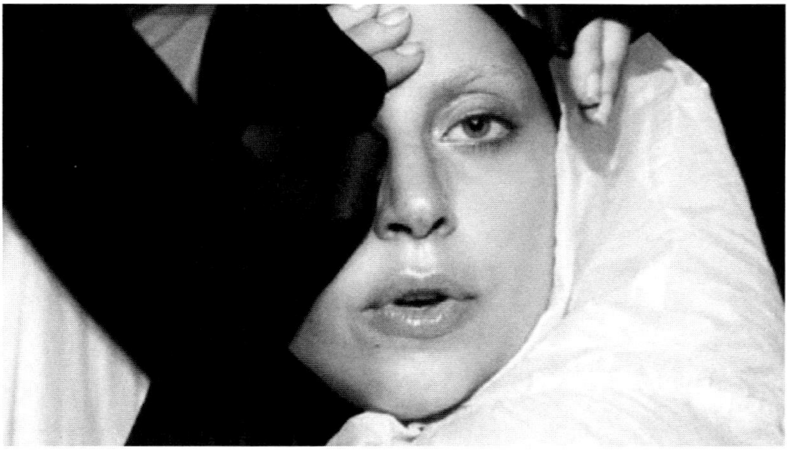

(Fig 3.9: Lady Gaga - Gaga meaning Pluto, 'god of the underworld', kindly demonstrating the 'eye of horus' symbol, so popular in modern celebrity culture)

Jesus healed the sick and the bible said in Colossians 1:17 ... *"and by him all things are held together"*.

When we look within the human body we have a magnificent system of self-healing called the Laminin. The Laminin, from where we get the word Laminate, is shaped like a cross and holds together tissue and muscles. It is also what the body uses to fight infection (more of this in the Moses story). This is Jesus holding all together and curing the sick, it is an internal system in the workings. The symbol of the Laminin is Lamb3 (3 = alpha, beta and gamma of the atom) and this is of course Jesus as the Lamb of God. We are brilliant beings of universal proportions and within us we have the microcosmic universe.

The story of Jesus is told by the gospels; Matthew, Mark, Luke and John, in other words the four elements and the four seasons which tell the story of the Sun throughout the year. The four gospels are the Tetramorph, four different and opposite elements merged together as one (the ancients believed god was the elements hence (EL-God) ements – Ment means mind). The bible also depicts this as the Eagle, Lion, Ox and the winged man, the four beasts.

(Fig 4.0: 'Tetramorph' - The four beasts)

The Archangels, Michael (Fire), Gabriel (Water), Raphael (Air) and Uriel (Earth) are also this depiction; the four elemets; in some faiths. They are also the 4 cardinal points, north, east, south and west and they tell the NEWS of Jesus. The word news being the letters of the compass points, n,e,s,w.

In figure 4.1, you will see 'the Last Supper' painting by Leonardo Da Vinci, who was Grand Master of the Priory of Sion (Sion = Sun). When you analyse the image you can clearly see the esoteric message. Jesus/Sun is in the middle of the disciples, also indicating their zodiac house; this is the Sun travelling through the 12 signs of the Zodiac (12 disciples). The disciples are positioned into 4 groups of 3; this is the seasons of the year, 3 months of spring, summer, autumn and winter. It is the story of Jesus, the Sun and its zodiac transit. He also painted the Mona Lisa, Mona meaning Moon and Lisa being L'isa, or Isis; in other words the Moon is Isis. The Sun and Moon are the two great luminaries.

(Fig 4.1: The esoteric meaning of 'The Last Supper' by Leonardo Da Vinci)

We spoke earlier about Judaism and the God Yahweh, this is relevant here too. John means Yahweh is gracious, Matthew means gift of Yahweh, and also Luke means light and Mark means designated to Mars, again planetary in nature.

Jesus was baptised like so many people of today and the past are. He was baptised by John the Baptist, the water bearer, or in zodiac terms, Aquarius, which exits visible sight below the equator upside down, hence John the Baptist was beheaded, in the biblical story.

The Life of Jesus: The zodiac Transit:

On December 25th each year the Sun moves 1 degree north to begin its annual transit, after 3 days, namely the 22nd/23rd/24th December within the same degree of sky, not moving; hence the Sun was dead for 3 days before it rose again (Easter connotations, or as stated in the bible "he rose early on the first day of the week", (that is referring to Sunday sunrise). Talking of Easter, East, Ost (dawn, to become light) where the sun rises, as I write this we have just entered April, the Nisan, where the sun rises over the equator, or in Judaic circles; the Passover, the sun passing over the equator itself, in Christianity this is the Sun/Son rise, when Jesus rose from the tomb.

(Fig 4.2: The hidden message within brand names and logos – This is the Passover)

On 25th December the Sun/Jesus is born by virtue of that 1 degree movement. This date may be quite important to many as they celebrate with gifts and enjoy family company each year, without knowing the astronomical relevance and origins of their efforts; it is Sun worship. In body universe terms Jesus is the messiah which means anointed, anointed means oil/oiled. To oil also means to impregnate which has other meanings other than the obvious to make pregnant, such as to lubricate, saturate or soak (pineal gland secretion/oil). The spinal fluid is the Christ solar seed/oil of Christ, that Mary, (the Ida within the brain) was impregnated with eventually leading to a 'virgin birth'. Ida = um = womb - in other words saturated by oil. After the crucifixion of the Christ seed (which is electrical charging by the Ida/Mary & Pingala/Joseph) it remains in the skull cavern (tomb/cerebellum) for 1 moon sign, the equivalent of 3 days; before it ascends to the pineal gland. Our spinal fluids contain Sodium Chloride, salt, Sal, we are our own salvation. The Ida is connected to the Moon and the Pingala is connected to the Sun; the masculine and feminine counterparts; the energy flow of the left and right hemispheres of the brain and through the human body and there we have Mary and Joseph and the solar seed, the christos, (Christ). The Pingala is Red and the Ida is blue, fire and water. It is again the wondrous workings of our bodies. Pingala = At = Ptah = Father.

And so the story of the life of Jesus has begun, he is the breath of life, which relates to Prana breathing a method of taking in sunlight at certain times such as sunrise and sunset, a human photosynthesis practiced by shamans and alike even today. He is the good shepherd, really this is the stars Alshat and Nashira, within the constellation of Capricorn, and they mean the sheep/flock.

We are taught that the life of Jesus was one of service and teachings, giving sermons on the mount and carrying out miracles such as the ones we have already mentioned. He was surrounded by his trusted disciples such as the one that kept all together, the Jew (Ju) Peter. This is of course another astronomical reference; this time it is the planet Jupiter; Piter/Peter = Petra = Petrol = Gas, and Jupiter the planet is a gas giant with a gravity so large it helps to keep our solar system together. It also protects Earth from space debris and meteors and alike.

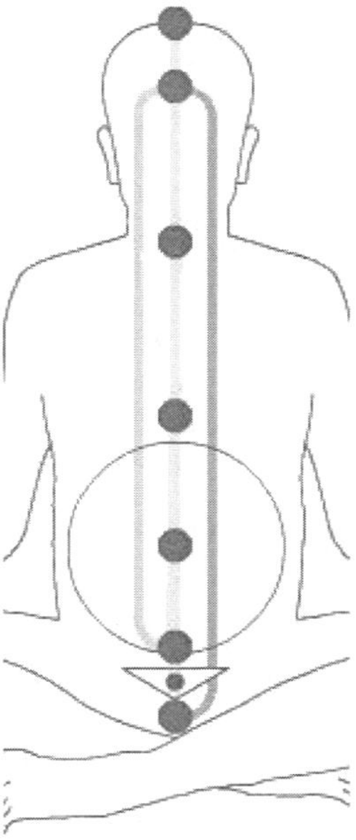

(Fig 4.3: Ida and Pingala)

As with all people who go against the system of rule, Jesus was betrayed by Judas and given a death sentence by the Romans. The people were given the choice, free Jesus or free Barabbas, they chose wrongly, symbolically this tells us that given the choice people choose wrong over right.

And so Jesus was nailed to the cross; (fire being a fixed sign) between the two thieves, the good thief and the bad thief, pending death by execution for our sins.

So what does this mean astronomically and also in a bodily counterpart? Let's start with astronomy.

The sun goes through each of the 12 zodiac signs in order to complete the year. It passes through Scorpio the back biter, the animal that hides in holes and waits for its opportunity to pounce and sting with its venom. This is Judas who betrayed Jesus by back stabbing him. The sun is then in a spiral towards its death, the winter, between the two thieves, the two solstices. The winter solstice is the bad thief as it steals the summer sun and the summer solstice is the good thief as it gives us the sun.

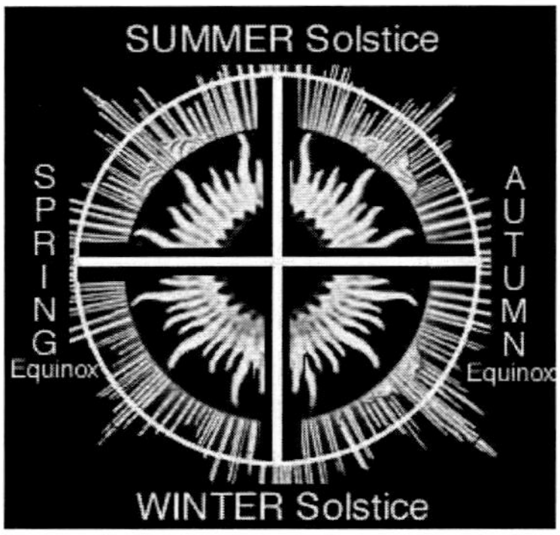

(Fig 4.4: This is Jesus/Sun on the cross,

(Fig 4.5: Short and long shadow of the cross)

The cross that we see on Churches is also in a physical sense, a representation of summer and winter. In the summer the sun is at a more direct angle and gives Earth a short shadow whereas in the winter the opposite occurs and we have the long shadow. See figure 4.5.

This is why the sign of the cross has one end longer than the other and not as you would expect; the standard letter T.

Above Jesus on the cross we have the letters 'INRI'; this represents the four elements in Latin:

Iam = Water
Nour = Fire
Ruach = Air
IABESHAH = Earth

When we add the Sun/Jesus, the fifth element by virtue of Yesod, the higher substance of light, we get the seal as in the Star of David, seal of Solomon. The four elements combined with the ether.

We are all born with original sin, we are born from light, an oscillation of the electromagnetic field and colour is the frequency of that oscillation. There is no other Sin, but the minds of people are controlled by its fake existence, fake in the religious sense and their teachings of deception.

Upon the crucifixion we are left with the blood of Christ, left by the nails positioned to form the Pentagram (Venus, morning star, which is sometimes associated with Jesus). The blood of Christ is really the red sky at sunset and sometimes sunrise:

(Fig 4.6: The Blood of Christ)

Now let's look at the bodily version of this story.

Within the human body we have an energy and chakra system (chakra meaning wheel in Sanskrit) that is believed to be the spiritual power of the human body. At the base of our spine, Jacob's ladder, we have a serpent energy called the Kundalini; again in Sanskrit this means the coiled one. The Kundalini is the energy of fire that climbs Jacob's ladder activating each of our energy centre's (Chakra's) on its way to the top. It destroys the lower chakras with its fire, the two lower chakra's are also known as Sodom and Gomorrah, based in the Kingdom of Earth, the lower body, as it approaches the Kingdom of Heaven, (Heaven meaning to heave up or to rise). Heaven is referring to the upper body, where the higher level chakras are situated. The lower Earth chakras are the lower density chakras, the cause of low vibrational desires such as sexual appetite etc, this is the destruction spoken about in the Bible, the fabled land of Sodom & Gomorrah destroyed by fire due to the fornication and seedy lifestyle of its inhabitants. Within the solar plexus, called Bethlehem, (which means house of bread), we have a Christ seed that is born (born in Bethlehem-Lord as in Lord Jesus originally meant the 'bread giver') and taken by our bodily fluids, salts, from where we get the word Sal (salvation) taking them to the father, the higher mind situated in the Cerebrum. Upon this approach the Christ seed is crucified by the electrical charges of the Ida and Pingala (Mary & Joseph) on the area of the brain known as the optic chiasm which was given the name the Crossing (X) by the Greeks. This is where the optic nerves partially cross below the Hypothalamus.

Therefore the Christ was crucified on the cross and returned to the father. We require a certain amount of these bodily fluids (salts) for this process to be successful, at least 10%; which is where we get the practice of the Tithe and celibacy, retaining the bodily fluids, within religious circles. Jesus died aged 33, which is also the number of the word Amen in gemetria, and also the numerical value of the 'Star of David. 33 is a numerological power number and numerology is a religion in itself for the shadow power Elites hence why such events as Armistace day ended at 6am on the 6th day of the 6th month (666) and the Great war ended on 11th hour of the 11th day of the 11th month, 11+11+11=33. Numerology is important and they use certain dates that harness the maximum energy for thier cause and this is also significant with the name of the biblical scripture numbers! And there you have it, Jesus went on to sit at the right hand side of the father in heaven; this is the Sun moving to the right hand side of the sky, (sky means heaven in many languages).

I have previously mentioned the other aspects of this occurrence in the Passover section (Christ seed and messiah/Oil and the tomb).

(Fig 4.7: Time lapse - 12 hours - 1 picture)

Fig 4.7 left, shows the Sun going to sit at the right hand side of the father – or for the Star wars fans out there, this is Luke (light) skywalker, Darth Vader meaning Dark Father, is Saturn and the Death star is Saturn's Moon; Mimas. And as for Princess Leah, well that was the name of Jacobs wife and that takes us firmly back to Judaism,Jacob of course had his name changed to Israel.

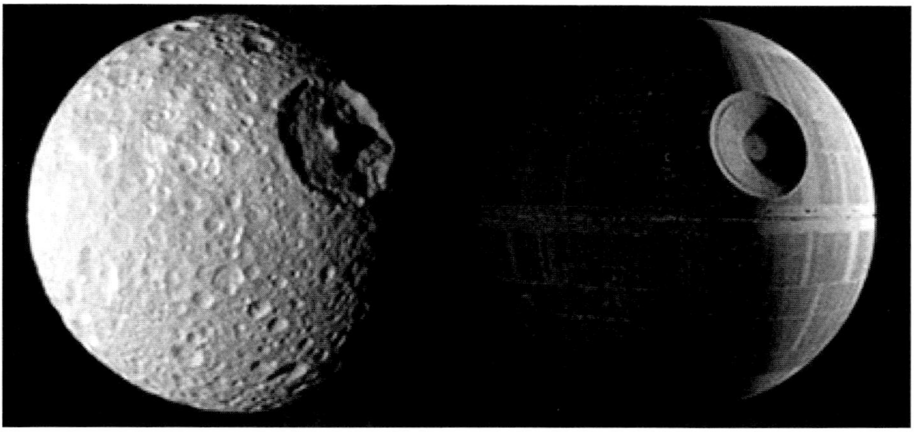

(Fig 4.8: (Left) Mimas, (Right) the Death Star)

We are our own Salvation and when we step out of spiritual darkness and into knowledge and the wisdom of the light we begin to realise this. This is the biblical story of Jonah and the whale, the whale was a symbol of spiritual darkness. And for the majority, even over 2000 years on; that darkness or putting it another way; ignorance; continues. When we start seeing ourselves as the only requirement we would have left behind the Old Testament and entered the New Testament, testament meaning body and mind.

It was once suggested to me that the Dead Sea Scrolls were proof that Jesus was a real person, but what is indeed true is that the Dead Sea Scrolls, or whatever is left of them, were found in the Qumran caves of an old settlement of the Pharasees, in the Judaean Desert of the West Bank, whom I have already mentioned had a hand in the deliberate mistruths of religious stories. Therefore this holds little credence.

Verse 1.6

MOSES

Another famous character of the bible is Moses found in a basket in the river and was raised by adoptive parents. Moses means ‘Drawn from the water’ and ‘Protection’ in other languages. He led the Israelites (Israel-Elites- Elite means Gods chosen ones) across the desert and took on the Pharaohs face to face demonstrating miracles; the most well-known being the parting of the red sea that then closed on the Egyptian army as they followed in pursuit. He climbed the Mountain of Sinai and spoke with God who gave him 10 commandments, the law, which he was to give to the people who had gathered and made the long journey across dessert sands, the long and lonely wilderness. Moses was also involved in the plagues of Egypt for example the death of the firstborn children at the hands of the angel of death et al. But again did this really happen in the physical biblical sense?

If thousands of people had made the exodus across the dessert and had lived there for 40 years then there would be physical evidence of this. No archaeologist and no Egyptologist have even found any artefacts or any physical remnants of such an odyssey. And there is a valid and simple reason for that, it didn’t happen. Again the whole story of Moses is a metaphor for the inner workings of genetics within the human body.

So let’s analyse the story itself.

Within the human body there is a water soluble protection around the cells of the body, this is called the ‘Fluid Mosaic Membrane’ Mosaic means Moses, drawn from the water. So straight away you can see that Moses was not a real person it is yet another story of human genetic origin.

Also within the body when a cell or aspect of DNA is dying it tells the other surrounding cells around it so that they can avoid any contamination. They give off a red dye (red blood on the doors of the houses of the first born to escape the angel of death) which is a message to them called Mito-genetic radiation or Mito Reds. Angel means messenger and this is the meaning of that particular scenario, that message of cellular or DNA death is the angel of death spoken about within this story. We have lots of protons in the body, they make up 1/3 of the atomic balance of our cells carried in our blood stream, or should we say Bourne, which means to be carried. Proton gives rise to proto, meaning first, therefore we have the First-Bourne (first born) again a genetic basis.

We have enzymes that open up the double helix strands of DNA and go inside them to help repair and fix the damaged or corrupted cells/DNA. Once inside; to prevent any other disease following behind the enzymes or even to escape the cleansing process; they close up the double helix strands behind the enzyme itself, in effect trapping them. This is what is described when the red sea closes in on the Egyptian army after they have entered the water to follow Moses and his people.

Now moving onto the rest of the story.

Moses scaled Mount Sinai until he reached the top awaiting any message or direction from God. What he saw was a burning bush which spoke to him giving him his 10 commandments which he was to take back to his people at the bottom of the mountain; Sinai incidentally comes from Sin, schin, and refers to the Moon (sinai = mountain of the Moon), the female aspect of Yesod. In Babylon Sin was the name of the Moon God. The burning bush is the pineal gland, our third eye, ignited by fire, the Kundalini energy; which we have previously mentioned. (Or in modern day computer logos, Mozilla Firefox, a fox being the symbol of spiritual awareness and Mozilla also means Moses) In Judaic circles Jacob fought the angel on mount Peniel and was shown the face of God, the Pineal gland, which this was referring to; is known as the face of God. Regardless of religion they are referring largely to the same subject.

The now globally famous 10 commandments, ment meaning mind, therefore to command the mind, were given to Moses on two stone plates which he was to later smash in anger, where we get the expression breaking or to break the law. Everyone knows the content of those commandments and what they are so we won't detail them here. However what is it actually referring to? Again this; as you would expect from a word containing mind; it is referring to the Brain. The stones are the two hemispheres of the human brain, the left and right side, the higher and lower mind (Taurus = Lower mind and Aries = higher mind, in medical astronomy). They are separated by cerebral fluids and blood, they are a red sea and to make the exodus from the lower to the higher mind we must cross the red sea... does this sound familiar?

The 10 commandments themselves are referring to the involution and evolution of conscience, the opposing currents of the hemispheres (masculine and feminine), 5+5 = 10 the number of male and female unity, the one (1) & the yoni (0) combined.

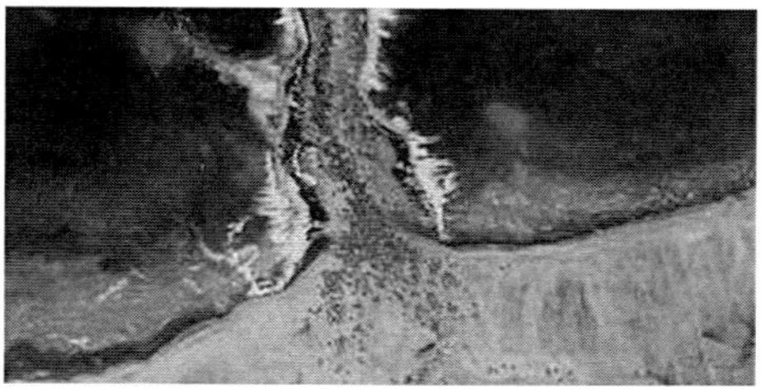

(Fig 4.9: Parting of The Red Sea)

Moses took the laws of God and brought them down the mountain to show the people and to tell them that this is how they should live their lives, to honour Gods law. When he saw them they were carving Bulls as fake Gods and this is when he smashed the tablets in anger at them. But what is this really telling us?

It is saying that humanity is operating in the lower mind (Taurus) and is not yet ready for the higher mind (Aries) and that is still relevant today when we see the actions of many and their mindless thought patterns of destruction and contempt. Those of the higher mind don't need laws they have a finely tuned conscience.

Verse 1.7
MEDICAL ASTRONOMY

** Medical astrology posits the association of each sign of the zodiac with parts of the body. The signs of the zodiac were believed to preside over the parts of the body, covering the body from head (Aries) to toe (Pisces), as follows:*

(Fig 5.0: Medical anatomy/astronomy and the Zodiac)

- Aries – head, face, brain, eyes
- Taurus – throat, neck, thyroid gland, vocal tract
- Gemini – arms, lungs, shoulders, hands, nervous system, brain
- Cancer – chest, breasts, stomach, alimentary canal
- Leo – heart, chest, spine, spinal column, upper back
- Virgo – digestive system, intestines, spleen, nervous system
- Libra – kidneys, skin, lumbar region, buttocks
- Scorpio – reproductive system, sexual organs, bowels, excretory system
- Sagittarius – hips, thighs, liver, sciatic nerve
- Capricorn – knees, joints, skeletal system
- Aquarius – ankles, circulatory system
- Pisces – feet, toes, lymphatic system, adipose tissue

The western astrology planets are also associated with certain portions and functions within the body:

The anatomical-astrological human

- Sun – heart, spine, and general vitality

(Author's note - Hence why we often see Jesus depicted with a large heart: It is also where we get historical characters such as Richard the Lionheart, which is the Sun in Leo, the Lion King (and the Elton John song, circle of life, referring to the zodiac, Elton incidentally means God's promise and John means Yahweh is gracious in Hebrew, these names are no coincidence in a world of secret languages)

(Fig 5.1: Jesus/Sun connected to the Heart – the hidden meaning of this picture)

- Moon – stomach, digestive system, female organs, lymphatic system
- Mercury – brain, central nervous system, thyroid gland, five senses, hands
- Venus – throat, kidneys, thymus gland, sense of touch, ovaries
- Mars – muscles, head, adrenal glands, senses of smell and taste
- Jupiter – liver, thighs, feet, growth, pituitary gland
- Saturn – skin, hair, teeth, bones, the body's defences, spleen
- Uranus – parathyroid gland, neural activity, aura
- Neptune – pineal gland, psychic healing
- Pluto – pancreas, metabolism, elimination

*(*Source – Wikipedia)*

We are the universe and we are the atoms and dust of the stars. We are connected in a much deeper way than most people will ever realise. Medical astronomy; the body universe; as above so below.

It is no surprise then that we are facing a multipronged attack from substances added deliberately to our food, water (such as fluoride which clogs and calcifies the pineal gland making it ineffective) air and medical treatments. There is a group of ruling elites that want to keep humanity firmly locked in a third dimensional reality and they know how to stifle spiritual development. Some time ago we looked into the work of a German biologist named Johanna Budwig who was able to cure cancer and other illnesses with good fats in their diet, the flaxseed diet to be exact. She also, as part of her research; discovered that our body's electrons love oxygen and as such they venture to the surface of our skin in order to get it. The Sun's photons are then able to partner those electrons and they marry together as a resonance energy system for solar energy, in addition to our bio-photons, the auric field. This then turns the body into a solar panel, a body of light in effect. It is needed for good health and also the spiritual development we previously briefly mentioned. We are given the likes of Sun-block which prevents this cycle from occurring, and again this is deliberate. The best remedy for sunburn is to be sensible, and take regular shade breaks. The pharmaceutical companies make customers not cures.

More information about Dr Budwig and her work can be found here:
www.budwigcenter.com

Verse 1.8

NOAH

Another world famous character of the bible was Noah, the man tasked with building a gigantic ark for all the animals of the world to board in order to be saved from the impending flood. He was to gather all the animals in two's; both male and female; so that they could procreate post flood and flourish the Earth once again. I often have mental images and one of those is of penguins packing their suitcases in Antarctica and waddling all the way to the Middle East to board the ark, of course unable to fly there. When you see things in this way you can then see the absurdity of the Noah story, but again only in the literal physical sense but not when you again attach a bodily connection to it, then it becomes very plausible. Noah means comfort and comfort and protection is what a baby; whist in its mother amniotic sack gets; protection from the outside world until the mother's waters flood.

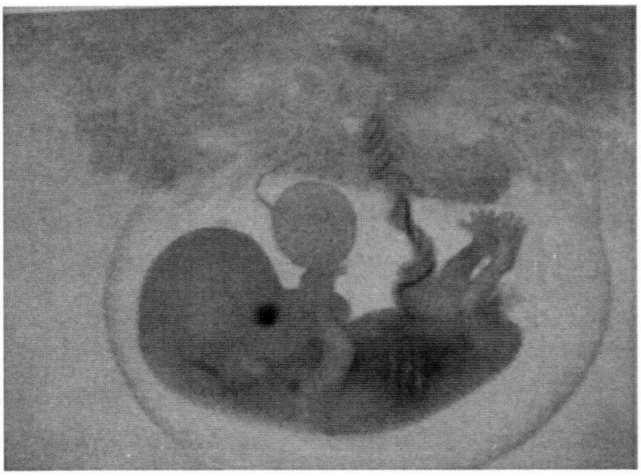

(Fig 5.2: Noah and the ark, comfort in the amniotic sac)

DNA is the building blocks of life and they are built upon base pairs, some genealogists actually call this miracle the 2 by 2 of chromosomes and this is what the story of the animals that went in two by two really means, it is the base pairs of human DNA.

Base pair - Dictionary Definition:

"A base pair is a unit consisting of two nucleobases bound to each

other by hydrogen bonds. They form the building blocks of the DNA double helix, and contribute to the folded structure of both DNA and RNA. Dictated by specific hydrogen bonding patterns, Watson-Crick base pairs allow the DNA helix to maintain a regular helical structure that is subtly dependent on its nucleotide sequence. The complementary nature of this based-paired structure provides a backup copy of all genetic information encoded within double-stranded DNA. The regular structure and data redundancy provided by the DNA double helix make DNA well suited to the storage of genetic information, while base-pairing between DNA and incoming nucleotides provides the mechanism through which DNA polymerase replicates DNA, and RNA polymerase transcribes DNA into RNA. Many DNA-binding proteins can recognize specific base pairing patterns that identify particular regulatory regions of genes"

It was not a titanic sized ship that was able to carry every species of animal, mammal and insect on the planet. Again it is talking about something much more simplistic, yet magnificent; the human body. As the baby leaves the womb during child birth it enters a new world post flood, after the breaking of its mother's flood waters where a new life begins. A mother's heartbeat, (the heart being an electromagnetic generator), is amplified within the amniotic sac. It is an electrical circuit which becomes more apparent when we analysis the word ar(k) the K is the symbol of an electrical circuit/relay and Biphasic electrical currents stimulate promoting both proliferation and differentiation of fetal neural stem cells. We are an electromagnetic computer. In much the same way that the Ark of the Covenant is the brain and its electrical system, covenant is a contract and that contract is with the higher mind (ment), which is a transmitter and receiver to a higher plane.

Verse 1.9

THE SUN`S CREATION OF OTHER EXISTENCES

I have briefly mentioned angels at various points in this book, I have also had experiences of seeing them myself in the form of colourful orbs at home and elsewhere and have even managed to take photographs of some of these orbs in a Rasha state of existence, (which is a pure light body to enable inter-dimensional passage through dimensional gateways.) Angels are significant in many of the world religions as messengers or protectors.

But what are these other worldly beings? The universal power is electromagnetic energy, male and female aspects; positive and negative charge enabled by dark matter; which acts like the neutron of an atom; which enables positive and negative opposites to co-exist without destroying themselves.

Angels are electromagnetic forces of consciousness able to navigate through electromagnetic field lines. The Sun is known as the 7 ray God and it is 7 colours that we are able to see within our human frequency spectra, in computing terms, our bandwidth. Those colours are the 7 colours of the Rainbow, or alternatively Ra-in-a-bow (RA = Sun in Egyptian – original meaning of arc was bow).

The angels are categorised into coloured rays and a rainbow is an angle of light, it is an archangel of light. Angle is an angel. God and his angle's = God and his Angels. The 7 rays are the 7 archangels, the 7 arch-angles that hit our brains receptors to be deciphered.

(Fig 5.3: Seven rays (Ra's) of the Archangels)

The solar sun's photons connect to human DNA by virtue of coded messages and frequencies; it is in itself another language of the genetic kind. As mentioned previously in this book angel means messenger, the informational codes of photon light are one such message.

Verse 2.0

SUN SYMBOLOGY IN BRAND NAMES AND LOGOS

The Sun is one of the highest levels of influence in our past and today. We see this hidden in plain sight by the secret language societies. We see it in company brand names and logos; we see it our newspaper titles and we see it in the form of animals such as the Lion, whose mane is symbolic of the rays of the Sun. But why the Lion?

A lion roars, when you look at the word roar backwards it is RA-OR; analysing the individual words Or is Gold and RA is the Egyptian Sun god, these words together mean 'golden Sun'.

The 'L' in lion is Ligand (Ligand dictionary definition) "which in coordination chemistry, a ligand is an ion or molecule that binds to a central metal atom to form a coordination complex. The bonding between metal and ligand generally involves formal donation of one or more of the ligand's electron pairs. The nature of metal-ligand bonding can range from covalent to ionic. The metal-ligand bond order can range from one to three Ions are an atom or molecule with a net electric charge due to the loss or gain of one or more electrons".

(Dictionary definition) - "The Ion is an atom or molecule with a net electric charge due to the loss or gain of one or more electrons. Deep in the Sun; electrons are torn free from atoms and these electrons absorb photons of light".

Words can sometimes tell a story in themselves. This process is also known as the 'Cobalt Complex' which gives off a blue pigment, cobalt blue is the colour associated with the Archangel Michael who is the soul essence of the Sun.

HIDDEN SUN SYMBOLS:

The word Symbol derives from Symbellon meaning a synchronicity, things joined together.

Sun worship is found in our daily life, corporate identities and brands. Even McDonalds' logo is a Sun symbol. Undoubtedly the Sun is worthy of such accolades as it is the reason we are able to exist on this planet during this incarnation. Without it nothing would exist here. The Sun is man's saviour - the golden orb that makes the dark and dangerous realm of the night disappear each morning. It enables each of us to see, feel warmth, and eat the offspring of its rays. Symbols are energetic and they connect to our sub-conscious mind in a suggestive way that can be positive or negative.

But how many have seen the esoteric Sun worship within many of the most famous locations in the world? Unless you have looked into the esoteric and are aware of this secret code, you may not be able to identify such symbols.

(Fig 5.4: Arch De Triumph, Paris)

Figure 5.4 (left) shows the famous Arch De Truimph in Paris from the air, with the Sun and its Rays blatantly obvious from this aerial view, usually unseen. It is situated in Champs Elysee, meaning *City of Light*, or *Sun*. Another famous Parisian landmark is the Eiffel tower which is itself a phallic symbol.

(Right, top) Figure 5.5 shows Number 10 Downing Street, London; British Prime Minister's residence. The Sun/flame of Nimrod is above the door accompanied by the number 10, which is a significant Sun number (Deccan). There are also Saturn symbols here too as well as the solar sun with the black door and black Lion (black sun) door knocker. Here we have both Sun and Saturn symbology at the heart of the British government...

(Fig 5.5: Prime Minister's residence, 10 Downing Street)

(Right) Figure 5.6 shows the Statue of Liberty in New York City, which is actually Isis, as that is who Liberty herself represents, holding the flame of Nimrod, the Babylonian Sun God. Geographically, Liberty faces Paris, which means 'the temple of Isis'. Her crown represents the Sun's rays.

(Fig 5.6: New York's 'Statue of Liberty' - Isis)

Figure 5.7 (overleaf) depicts the memorial of Princess Diana, Pont De Alma, Paris. Pont De Alma means 'Bridge of the Soul' it is situated on top of an ancient sacrificial location for sacrifices to the goddess Diana, no coincidence.

As the theme of this book indicates, religion is the worship of stars and planets and numerology and astronomy are the religions of the world's ruling elites. And it is to this end that many ground breaking events take place at certain significant times of planetary alignment or movement.

(Fig 5.7: Pont De Alma and the flame of Nimrod, Paris)

With this in mind let's look a little more into the death of Princess Diana and also 9/11 from this perspective.

Princess Diana died at 22:27 (GMT) 2+2+2+7= 13, she crashed into the 13th pillar. At the time of the incident 3 planets were in the 4th house of astronomy, Moon, Mercury & the Sun, (3 people died in the crash) the 4th house of astronomy is known as the Grave, and it is concerned with hidden things, private affairs and most significantly the ultimate end and aim of terrestrial existence. She died on 31st August, 3+1 = 4 (4th house) on Saturday (Saturn's day). Again this is astronomical evidence that all is not as it has been portrayed.

Now dealing with 9/11; When the twin towers were built in 1970, Saturn was in Gemini, the twins, as in twin towers. When the towers were brought down in 2001 Saturn had just completed its thirty year orbit and was again in Gemini. When the first plane hit, Saturn was in the 8th house of astronomy, the place of highest potential and when the second plane hit, Saturn was going into the 8th house of astronomy, the house of death.

When Samson the ancient protector of Israel brought down the Philistine towers he killed 3000 Canaanites. When Uncle Sam, the current protector of Israel brought down the twin towers, they killed just less than 3000, only 4 short. The London 7/7 bombings were committed with Israeli significance too, 77 is the 'Revenge of Lamech', the punishment of the Biblical Cain's relative, Lamech, 77 fold. Those who punish Cain will be punished 7 times more, those who punish Lamech will be punished 77 times more according to the Hebrew scriptures; a statement made by the Hebrew God. And then returning to 9/11 and the 77 numerology relating to that too. During the incident we had flight 77, floor 77 of the South tower was hit by the second plane and the Pentagon is situated 77 degrees Western latitude. When such events occur always look what the planets are doing to find the hidden meaning.

Numerology has been used since ancient times and the likes of dice and dominos were originally used for fortune telling by numbers. And when we see the information such as above then anyone with even the slightest ounce of an open mind can see it could have been no coincidence, instead it was carefully planned and orchestrated from within based on significant numbers to maximise the energetic impact of the event/agenda.

In terms of the name Paris; it means Temple of Isis, Isis is another name for the goddess Diana. Again, the flame of Nimrod; the Sun god in Babylonian; has been erected.

Many more obelisk symbols exist around the world in such places as the Vatican, Washington, D.C. and the City of London. And each is a secret code for those with eyes to decipher.

Even at the heart of British government at the "Houses of Parliament" in London, we have "Big Ben", which is really a phallic symbol. It is the penis of Osiris the Egyptian Sun god, and "Ben" is simply the benbenet which is the pyramid cap.

(Fig 5.8: Houses of Parliament, London)

So next time you are out and about, keep one eye on the symbols - the secret language around you. It can be very interesting indeed!

Now let's look at such symbols within a few of the most well-known brands and logos and media. There are too many to list here but here are a few of the best examples.

(Fig 5.9: McDonalds symbology)

McDonalds: The Golden 'M' is the Sun; symbolic of the archways at the entrance to the temple of Solomon (Sol-Om-On). Ronald McDonald is a Masonic Shriner clown and McDonalds itself means Mac (son) Dom-Nuill; all together meaning, Sun, ruler of the world. The red and yellow colours are sunrise and sunset. Sideways the logo is the number 13, the number of perfect heavenly government, Jesus (Sun) + 12 disciples (Zodiac) = 13.

(Fig 6.0: Shell Petrol logo)

Shell Petrol: This is Venus who was birthed out of a shell. Venus's light is a reflection of Sunlight, hence the solar glow around the symbol.

(Fig 6.1: BP logo)

BP: This is the symbol of the Sun in the centre and also Wadjet, the Egyptian cat goddess associated with the sun. Wadjet was the protector of Royal women and Wadjet day is celebrated on 21st April, which is also the Queen of England's birthday. Again no coincidence.

(Fig 6.2: The Black Sun)

IHS: This is the black sun which can also be seen at the Vatican. The black sun is Saturn which has been mentioned many times throughout these pages.

NEWSPAPERS:

The Evening Star.

No. 14,184. WASHINGTON, D. C., SATURDAY, JUNE 18, 1898—TWENTY-FOUR PAGES. TWO CENTS.

GEN. MILES' COURSE

TOO MUCH RED TAPE

(Fig 6.3: The Evening Star Newspaper)

The Evening Star: (Also known as the Morning star) which is Venus, and also Lucifer in various circles.

(Fig 6.4: The Sun Newspaper)

The Sun: This is the UK's most popular newspaper, the Sun, no prizes for guessing what this represents! The main area of the press in London is in Fleet Street. Fleet means 'under the same ownership', which is correct of the media. It is all owned by the same elite family base, giving us one version of events; their version.

CAR LOGOS:

(Fig 6.5: Mazda car logo)

Mazda: This is an ancient Sun symbol of the Iraqi religion Zoroastrian, the battle of light and dark (also relevant to the movie and character - Zoro).

(Fig 6.6: Subaru car logo)

Subaru: Meaning the Pleiades, which is a constellation and also believed to be the home of a Nordic looking race of Extraterrestrials.

(Fig 6.7: Toyota car logo)

Toyota: This logo is Venus being penetrated by Mars with Earth as the surrounding circle; it is also very similar looking to the female reproductive organs.

(Fig 6.8: vauxhall car logo)

Vauxhall: The Griffin, a combination of a Lion and an Eagle; two sun symbols, two energies merged.

COMPUTING

(Fig 7.0: Acer logo)

(Fig 6.9: Dell logo)

On these two examples above, of many I could have chosen, we see the letter 'E' is more prominent than the others having emphasis placed on it. The letter E is the fifth letter of the alphabet and is significant of the fifth element, the ether, the higher light. Even the word five; when broken down is significant too. Fi (Phi = geometric maths to the number 5), V (five in Roman numerals) and E as just stated is the ether, fifth element = FIVE.

The list is really endless, we could go on with logo after logo but by now you would have gotten the general gist. Our whole reality field is created for us and hidden symbols and meanings are a language around us in everyday life that we do simply not see. And we don't see it because we have not trained ourselves to see it. The initiates see it and they respond to it, as does our sub-conscious. Learn the language and speak the part and open up a brand new world for yourselves and others. It is said that we sub-consciously see around 1000 of these symbols each day.

Verse 2.1

"MY FATHER`S HOUSE HAS MANY ROOMS"

The title of this verse is yet another deep and meaningful quote attributed to Jesus but which has a far reaching esoteric meaning.

We are multi-dimensional beings, we are existing in just one octave of an endless universe, the third dimension, or at least this one aspect of our true essence is. When we look at the third dimension from elsewhere we see a greater viewpoint, we step out of the 3D realm for that moment in time.

There is more than one universe, there are possibly many. Third dimensional space is height, length and width married with time, a fourth dimensional entity to give us time and space, our reference of sequential movement, a measurable reference point that enables us to judge distance, movement and our speed. Time is the duration of existence; all things are sewn together by the connecting strings of linear time. There has to be a definitive separation of each third dimensional static block, this is the interim time and space we know as the life and death cycle. When we take a photograph for example we freeze time, it becomes 0 time, static forever, outside of linear time motion.

This is necessary otherwise there would be no dimensions there would be only singular existence from where we all originated, the one, the cause; with an effect we call duality, yin and yang, opposite polarity, we are really a trinity of cosmic proportions. We don't often sense or see or even know about linear time until something changes to throw you off your straight line, the mundane, and the routine passage through life. That change then replaces linear time with lateral time; we have a different view, even a different viewing speed within the multiple frames of our life movie, frame by frame until the film is completed. This fluctuation in the matrix shows us that there are many realities, even parallel universes that we catch a glimpse of, Deja vue, but in fact this is seeing another time line. The past and present are within the same space, as Einstein expressed it, if you put a smaller box into a larger box they are separate entities occupying the same area of space, this is a description of many dimensions. The future is in a position on the linear time line not activated until the now reaches it but it is still in the same area of space. The faster we travel the more time is distorted; this was proven in a scientific experiment called 'Time Dilation' which was conducted by scientist Carol Allie at Maryland University, USA, in the 1970's. For this experiment she timed someone at ground level and also in a fighter jet at the same time, the two times distorted when speed was introduced. This is how when someone is taken from Earth (alien abduction for example) at speed, time on Earth stays the same speed, however for the one traveling away at speed time has changed, hence why they have lost hours even days of time when they return.

Like all laws, this time the law of physics, there is a speed limit that controls the level of speed of change within our conscious realm of existence; this is the speed of light. In effect we have been capped. The fluctuation of change cannot exceed the speed of light, so for us nothing can go faster, albeit there are things that can such as partiki particles, luminous sub-atomic particles that can be viewed in spiritual terms as units of the identity of God, the central creative source. They are outside of these laws.

My father's house, the universe or multiverse, has many rooms, in other words, it has many dimensions and many different frequencies of existence. Just like our house has a living room, kitchen, bedrooms and so on within the same area of space and time, separated by walls which hide them from sight, universal walls are frequency and vibration that control our frequency spectra and we see less than 1% of it. So just ask yourself what is in the 99% we cannot see?

But like all walls they have windows and from those windows we can see other places. We are not alone, we are one particle of billions and our magnitude is of universal proportions. When this is known, there is no need for war, religion; famine, greed or infighting, or separation; we are all one. Petty squabbles are reduced to insignificance. We are human, meaning that we are supernatural gods.

Keep progressing and moving forwards, as the saying that came into my mind states "*Time stands still for no man; otherwise he'd be a photo*".

Verse 2.2

THE FINAL VERSE - A NEW TESTAMENT

In conclusion; in this book we have covered Christianity, Judaism, Islam, Catholicism, and other main religions of the world. We have seen how the stories contained within the scriptures are multi-level with the masses, the general populous; getting only a superficial version; a story; which covers up a greater and deeper truth, the fact that we are brilliant individuals who are part of a larger existence as our name Human suggests.

(Fig 7.1: Greater Israel)

We have covered symbols within buildings and famous brand names and logos and how they are a secret language of the initiates as a means of Mudra, a public symbolic language only they understand, seemingly laughing at the ignorance of the many; is this because they enjoy our slavery and humiliation? When you look into some of the documented statements from members of the ruling family 'elites', that would appear correct.

We have covered how the majority of things practiced and acted out in our society today has an astronomical basis or even a genetic base too.

Even our beloved historical characters are in the stars, they are the stars and planets. Even King Arthur, who hasn't appeared in this book, is of astrological base. Arthur is Artos which means Bear, the constellation 'The bear'. Pendragon means 'Dragon Master' and this is the constellation of Draco, meaning Dragon. Avalon derives from Avaloch meaning apple, the symbol of magical transformation. And the sword, as in Excalibur; is symbolic of impenetrable knowledge; accessed only by the selected few; hence why Arthur was the only who could remove the sword from the stone. Camelot means Arthurs castle and a castle is a fortified building, Merlin means Sea fortress and he is wizard which is a synonym of star and within the constellation of the Plough; which forms part of the Great Bear constellation; we have in the handle 3 stars called the Wizard's march. Merlin is in Earth terms the fortress of Arthur's castle but it also has the astronomical theme as does everything. Tintagel is built on a fortress. Excalibur derives from Ex calce liberatus, "liberated from the stone" and in the Jewish kabbalah the pineal gland is known as the Foundation Stone, the liquid of life (lake) in other words the sword was taken from the stone, the knowledge is taken from the pineal gland; by the chosen, in this story only Arthur could remove the sword. The round table is the circular zodiac wheel with the 12 knights being the 12 zodiac characters.

As briefly hinted there is an underlying ruling elite on planet Earth who have their own agenda of control. It is in their interest and the interests of that agenda to have the global population at war and at odds in order to deflect from what is going on behind the scenes. Much of the agenda is a Zionistic desire for a greater Israel, the Promised Land.

This is the region of many wars as this agenda is fulfilled. Many cite the likes of the Rothschild's and Rockefeller families as being the main men, however we know about these so this indicates that they are not, although very high in the pecking order. The ones really at the helm are hidden and not known, some even suggest that they are not even from our planet. They hide the truth and give you their version of history to remain in control. They talk publically amongst themselves with mudras and privately with initiations. They control the minds of the people and they control our 'version' of reality. People are taught from birth to accept and not to question. Instead of endless gods why not just believe in ourselves, no more Eiledon? We are superhuman consciousness, awareness that has become unaware. Unaware of itself and unaware of our real potential. When we become aware once again we are a threat to a system that has closed us down at our every level and at our very essence.

I have no doubt that there are energy manifestations of some kind and we experience that through the countless channellings and channellers. I also have no doubt that these channellers are invoking a third dimensional aspect of the energy they call, which then morphs into a pre-conceived format. But as for the physical people mentioned in the bible and alike the evidence in this book and my personal opinion indicates that they are nothing more than a work of fiction.

I am also very aware that part of the so called New World Order (NWO) agenda is to attack and turn against religion, replacing it with a one world religion which is the religion of the ruling power elites (on the face of it this may sound like a good thing, but the intention and possible conclusion to this agenda is not a good thing). I am also aware that books such as this one would seemingly aid that agenda. However that is not the intention and moreover it has been written to make people aware of fact rather than the usual mistruths that cloud our judgement and knowledge base. It is a Revelation, which is also the last book of the bible which means 'The divine or supernatural disclosure to humans relating to human existance or disclosure of some form of truth or knowledge' the information in this book is that Revelation. Revelation also talks about the 4 horsemen of the apocalypse, the end times; it is again talking about the infuence of the planets, the white horse (Venus) the Red horse (Mars), the Black horse (Saturn) and the Pale horse (Pluto/hades).

An apocalypse, translated literally from Greek, is 'through the concealed', meaning a disclosure of knowledge, i.e., a lifting of the veil or revelation. In religious contexts it is usually a disclosure of something hidden,this book is also your apocalypse. And ask yourself this question, why would God, the pure mathematician of creation with all its infinite fractals and duplification have only 'one' begotten son? On the basis of the story dold to us It makes no sense at all.

I hope that this book has inspired you and many others to continue with the pursuit of secret teachings and hidden knowledge. For whatever reason you are reading it, it is meant; you are at that place of yearning, yearning for truth.

For me, the research and learning continues with each day, it has become a passion to seek answers, I won't find them all, but I will at least try...

Best wishes and good luck.

• • •

PISCES
ARIES
TAURUS
GEMINI
CANCER
LEO
VIRGO
LIBRA
SCORPIO
SAGITTARIUS
CAPRICORN
AQUARIUS

INRI

CAPRICORN
SAGITTARIUS
SCORPIO
LIBRA
VIRGO
LEO
CANCER

PISCES
ARIES
TAURUS
GEMINI
CANCER
LEO
VIRGO
LIBRA
SCORPIO
SAGITTARIUS
CAPRICORN
AQUARIUS

* 9 7 8 0 9 9 5 4 5 5 4 5 0 *

WS - #0065 - 010421 - C6 - 229/152/6 - PB - 9780995455450 - Gloss Lamination